NINE LIVES

NINE LIVES
Cats in Folklore

Katharine M. Briggs

with illustrations by John Ward, RA

Routledge & Kegan Paul
London and Henley

First published in 1980
by Routledge & Kegan Paul Ltd
39 Store Street, London WC1E 7DD and
Broadway House, Newtown Road,
Henley-on-Thames, Oxon RG9 1EN
Set in Bembo 11 on 13pt by
Rowland Phototypesetting Ltd, Bury St Edmunds, Suffolk
and printed in Great Britain by
Unwin Brothers Ltd
The Gresham Press, Old Woking, Surrey
A member of the Staples Printing Group

British Library Cataloguing in Publication Data

Briggs, Katharine Mary
Nine lives.
1. Cats (in religion, folk-lore, etc.)
I. Title
398'.369'974428   GR725

ISBN 0 7100 0638 1

This book is for Katharine Law,
who taught my Rollo to be happy
with dogs

Contents

Acknowledgments

The author and publishers acknowledge the following for permission to reprint previously published material:

B. T. Batsford, for excerpts from *Folklore of the Lake District* by Marjorie Rawling, and *The Folklore of East Anglia* by Enid Porter; from the series edited by Venetia Newall.

Blackstaff Press, for excerpts from *Now You're Talking*, by Michael J. Murphy.

The Bodley Head and Macmillan Publishing Co., for excerpts from *The Last Battle*, by C. S. Lewis. Copyright © 1956 by C. S. Lewis.

W. & R. Chambers, for excerpts from *New Tales from Grimm*, translated by Ruth Michaelis-Jena and Arthur Ratcliff.

Dobson Books, for excerpts from *The Stone Cage* and *Over the Hills to Fabylon* by Nicholas Stuart Gray.

John Farquharson, for excerpts from *Miss Kelly*, by Elizabeth Holding, published by Michael Joseph.

Grove Press, for excerpts from *Folktales from Korea*, by Zong-in-Sob.

Haldanes McLaren and W. S. Scott, for excerpts from *A Forgotten Heritage*, by Hannah Aitken.

George G. Harrap, for excerpts from *West Indian Folk Tales* by Lucille Iremonger.

Houghton Mifflin, for 'The Two Lost Babes,' from *Grandfather Tales*, by Richard Chase. Copyright 1948 by Richard Chase, copyright © renewed 1976 by Richard Chase.

Hutchinson, for excerpts from *Encyclopedia of Superstitions*, by E. and M. A. Radford.

Acknowledgements

Alfred A. Knopf, Inc., for 'The Cat's Baptism', from *The Magic Orange Tree and Other Haitian Folktales*, collected by Diane Wolkstein and illustrated by Elsa Henriquez. Copyright © 1978 by Diane Wolkstein.

The Literary Estate of Sylvia Townsend Warner and Chatto & Windus, for excerpts from *Lolly Willowes*, by Sylvia Townsend Warner.

The Society of Authors as the literary representatives of the Estate of John Masefield and Macmillan Publishing Co., for excerpts from *Midnight Folk*, by John Masefield.

The Society of Authors as the literary representatives of the Estate of Walter de la Mare for excerpts from *Broomsticks*, by Walter de la Mare.

Ulster Tatler for excerpts from 'Heart of Down', by E. M. Griffith.

University of Chicago Press for excerpts from the series *Folktales of the World*, edited by Richard M. Dorson.

Frederick Warne for excerpts from *The Tailor of Gloucester* by Beatrix Potter. Copyright © F. Warne & Co., Ltd, London and New York.

1

The Cult of the Cat and the Cat Goddess

The great day for the cat must be placed some two thousand years ago in Ancient Egypt, when cats enjoyed a position of special privilege, and had long held it. The cat goddess was Bast, who was generally shown as a female figure with a cat's head but sometimes assumed the form of a gigantic cat. Bubastis was the original home of Bast, but after a time the cat became a sacred character through the whole of Egypt, which indeed appears to have been a nation of fanatical animal-lovers.[1]

As we shall see, there is a good deal of evidence to show that cats were regarded as supernatural creatures in many places that were far removed from Egypt, but the difference between the Egyptian view of cat character and that of general tradition is very striking. As a rule one would regard cats as nocturnal animals, and we do a certain violence to their nature when we try to make them keep us company during the day and settle down to sleep comfortably in the house at night. It is a little surprising to find that the goddess Bast was a sun deity when one would have expected her to be attached to the moon and to darkness. However, it was so.

The Egyptians have given us very little precise information about their numerous Pantheon, and, except for what we can glean from the *Book of the Dead*, we rely for a great deal of our knowledge upon the Greek historians and travellers, Herodotus, Diodorus Siculus and Plutarch. Because of this we have very little information about the early worship of the sacred animals. It seems likely that they were originally totem animals, then perhaps local deities, and that the cult of some of them, and among these the cat, spread all over Egypt. Cats, though they were domestic pets, not exclusively temple animals, were universally sacred, and anyone who killed a cat, even accidentally, was put to death. According to the account given by Diodorus, cats, hawks, and ibises were the most ardently protected of the sacred animals. Diodorus Siculus, who was born about 100 BC, gives a vivid account of this. He writes:

> When one of these animals is concerned, he who kills one, be it accidentally or maliciously, is put to death. The populace flings itself on him, usually before he can be tried and judged. Superstition towards these sacred animals is deeply rooted in the Egyptian's soul, and devotion to their cult is passionate. In the days when Ptolemy Auletes was not yet allied to the Romans, and the people of Egypt still hastened to welcome all visitors from Italy, and, for fear of the consequences, care-fully avoided any occasion for complaint or rupture, a Roman killed a cat. The populace crowded to the house of the Roman, who had committed the 'murder'; and neither the efforts of the magistrates sent by the King to protect him nor the universal fear inspired by the might of Rome, could avail to save the man's life, though what he had done was admitted to be accidental. This is not an incident which I report from hearsay, but something I saw myself during my sojourn in Egypt.[2]

Diodorus also gives us some pleasant details of social history about these pet cats. They were fed on bread-and-milk, and slices of Nile fish, and they were summoned to their meals by certain set calls. For all we know it may have been an equivalent of 'Pussie, Pussie, Pussie'! After their death their bodies were carefully embalmed.[3] Lewis Spence quotes a passage from Herodotus, written some four centuries earlier, which gives much the same picture.

When a conflagration takes place a supernatural impulse seizes upon the cats. For the Egyptians, standing at a distance, take care of the cats and neglect to put out the fire; but the cats, making their escape, and leaping over the men, throw themselves into the fire; and when this happens great lamentations are made among the Egyptians. In whatsoever house a family cat dies a natural death all the family shave their eyebrows only, but if a dog dies they shave their whole body and the head. All cats that die are carried to certain sacred houses, where, being first embalmed, they are buried in the city of Bubastis.[4]

The truth of this has been confirmed by later excavations. The return to the original home of the cult suggests that the connection with the goddess Bast was still close even at this late period. In a late Demotic papyrus cited by Lewis Spence, there is a lively discussion between the goddess Bast in the form of a gigantic cat and a small jackal who seems to represent a trickster figure. The cat takes the positive side of the argument. She maintains that the gods are in charge of the universe and that right will triumph in the end; a man who ill-treats even a little lamb will suffer for it, the clouds that overshadow ill-used creatures will roll away and innocence will be vindicated. The jackal, however, is a pessimist. He points out that the lizard devours the fly, the bat eats the lizard and is swallowed by the snake, which is pounced upon by the hawk. In fact the whole of nature is at war. The dispute becomes heated and is enlivened by anecdotes and proverbs. It seems as if the author's sympathy is with the jackal, but unfortunately the papyrus is mutilated and we never hear the end of the argument.[5]

Bubastis was at one time the capital of Egypt, and it was then that the local cat-cult spread over the whole country. Bast reached the height of her popularity in the fourth century BC. She was a goddess of pleasure and music and especially of the dance, and would beat time to music with the sistrum held in her hand. Herodotus gives us an enthusiastic account of the great annual festival held at Bubastis in honour of the goddess. Her temple was one of the most elegant in Egypt, and pilgrims came from all over the country to attend it, travelling in barges, alive with the sound of castanets, and flutes, with dance, song and merriment. The pilgrims exchanged quips with the women who ran to the banks of the Nile to watch them pass. Hundreds and thousands came to the great fair, and on the sacred day a glittering procession wound its way through the streets to the temple and more wine was drunk in the festivities that followed than in all the rest of the year. It is true of course that a large proportion of the population of the country was in the town on that day.[6]

Bast was not only a sportive goddess, but a benevolent one, and a healer of disease. There were many demons and sinister powers in the Egyptian mythology, but she was always beneficent. Some faint memory of these healing qualities may have clung to the cat's traditions even in the darker days that were to come, for, as we shall see later, some strange magical properties were ascribed to different parts of the cat's body and used to make grisly remedies.

When we leave Africa, and move North into the very different mythology of Scandinavia, we find that the cat has acquired another patron. Freyja, the Scandinavian goddess of fertility, of beauty, love and marriage, adopted the cat as one of her cult animals, and when she did not ride her horse into battle she travelled in a chariot drawn by cats.

Grimm, in his *Teutonic Mythology*, suggests that the sinister strain in the cat traditions may have been due to Freyja's ambivalence as at once the patroness of lovers and the chooser of the slain, and hostess to the dead in her high and spacious palace in Asgard. This may have had its effect, but the spread of Christianity is the more likely cause.[7]

The early Christian missionaries to Europe acted wisely and lovingly in presenting the positive aspect of Christianity to their converts and christianizing heathen holy days and sacred places. The Roman Saturnalia settled happily into Christmas, the Teutonic Eostre was reshaped to celebrate the Resurrection, many heathen temples blossomed afresh as Christian churches, Bride, the Celtic goddess of spring and mating, was adopted as St Bridget of Ireland. Even a mermaid was successfully canonized as St Libyan.[8] But when whole tribes and nations were carried over by their rulers and baptized willy-nilly they inevitably brought a great deal of undigested heathenism with them. The grimmer gods and goddesses, probably those to whom extensive sacrifices were made, took demonic forms, and some among them were cat goddesses. The Cailleach Bheur of the Scottish Highlands, the Blue Hag of Winter, who sometimes appeared in cat form, was one of them. She was a nature goddess, who herded the deer as her cattle. The touch of her staff drove the leaves off the trees, and brought snow and harsh weather. When spring came she threw her staff away under a holly tree and took the shape of a standing stone until the autumn.[9] A tale was told of her in her cat form that resembles Grant Stewart's 'Legend of the Witch of Laggan'.[10]

Another cat demon of Britain is Black Annis of the Dane Hills in Leicestershire, who was probably a descendent of the Celtic Danu, one of the goddesses of war. "In *The County Folk-Lore of Leicestershire* Charles James Billson goes into the traditions of Black Annis at some length, quoting from various sources.[12] Among them he gives an extract from Dudley's *Naology*.[13] He describes the cave, about a mile from Leicester, where there is a series of low hills called the Dane Hills. For many centuries this was a wild forest. He goes on:

> On the side of one of the knolls in this formerly wild district was a round cave, of diameter of ten or twelve feet, and height about five, excavated from the sandstone strata then extant. This cave was known by the name of *Black Annis's Bower*. Black Annis was said in the county to have been a savage woman with great teeth and long nails, and that she devoured human victims . . . . The name of Annis, to whom this cave is said to belong, is known to the Celtic mythologist by the name of *Anu* or *Nannu*, names signifying the mother goddess, according to the authority of Vallancey, an author well learned in the Celtic language of the Irish.

Little children who went to run on the Dane Hills, were assured that she (Black Annis) lay in wait there, to snatch them away to her 'bower'; and that many like themselves she had 'scratched to death with her claws, sucked their blood, and hung up their skins to dry'.

Billson supplements this with several quotations from the *Leicester Chronicle* of 1874.

Black Anna was said to be in the habit of crouching among the branches of the old pollard oak (the last remnant of the forest) which grew in the cleft of the rock over the mouth of her cave, or 'bower', ever ready to spring like a wild beast on any stray children passing below. The cave she was tradition-ally said to have dug out of the solid rock with her finger nails.[14]

To these is added a note by Miss Henrietta Ellie.

A relic of this still remains in the minds of people in Leicester in the form of 'Cat Anna'. Some warehouse girls told me a short time ago that she was a witch who lived in the cellars under the castle, and that there was an underground passage from the cellars to the Dane Hills, along which she ran.[15]

Long before these accounts were written Black Annis's memory had been celebrated by the Easter Monday Drag Hunt. The bait was a dead cat soaked in aniseed and it was drawn from Black Annis's Bower by devious ways through the city till it ended at the mayor's house. This was attended in the Dane Hills on Easter Monday morning by great numbers of people, who climbed the various knolls to watch the hunt. The Mayor entertained a large company when the hunt was over. The hunt itself gradually dwindled away from about 1767, though an Easter Monday Fair was kept up in the Dane Hills for some time after that. The first mention of it in the town records is in 1668, but it is described there as very ancient.[16]

The hag, Black Annis, however, was still remembered at the time of the Second World War. Ruth Tongue has recorded a vivid story told her by a little evacuee from Leicester in which Black Annis was providentially destroyed.

Black Annis
Black Annis lived in the Danehills.

She was ever so tall and had a blue face and had long white teeth and she ate people. She only went out when it was dark.

My mum says, when she ground her teeth people could hear her in time to bolt their doors and keep well away from the one window. That's why we don't have a lot of big windows in Leicestershire cottages, so she can't only get an arm inside.

My mum says that's why we have the fire and chimney in a corner.

The fire used to be on the earth floor once and people slept all round it until Black Annis grabbed the babies out the window. There wasn't any glass in that time.

When Black Annis howled you could hear her five miles away and then even the poor folk in the huts fastened skins across the window and put witch-herbs above it to keep her away safe.

My mum told us there was a wicked stepmother who sent her three little children out near Christmastide to gather wood when it got dark earlier than this is (a dark lunchtime, Christmas Eve 1941). They were ever so cold and frightened and little Dicky he cried.

'Don't cry, Dicky lad,' says Jim. 'Don't be frightened. 'Tis Christmas Eve. You can't be hurted nowaries.'

'Why?' says Dicky.

'There's no bad 'uns about,' says Jen.

'Why?' says Dicky.

''Tis Our Lord's birthday and the bells ring,' they said. 'If the bad 'uns hear them they die.'

So off they went to the wood and picked a big load each. It was getting dark and they had a long way back and they were so tired and little Dicky cried and so did Jen. 'It's getting dark and she may not have gone under the earth yet. I'm going to run.'

But she couldn't with all her load of firewood.

Then Jim said, 'I've got a holed stone and if you like I'll look through it and see. But she'll be right underground with the covers over her ears till after Christmas.'

But she wasn't, she'd forgotten the day and Jim saw her five miles off.

It wasn't quite dark yet and they tried to make haste. Then Jim looked again. 'She's only a mile away,' he whispered, but they couldn't go any faster until they heard a yell.

Then they did run till they dropped.

'She won't come now,' says Jim. 'She'll stop to eat that ragged, drunken old woman I saw – I think it was Step-mother come to look for us.'

'I hope it were,' says Jen and little Dicky. 'We're nearly home now.'

So they rested just a bit longer and then little Dicky says, 'It's coming on near dark' and Jen says, 'There's something grinding teeth. Look through the stone, Jim.'

So Jim looked and it was Black Annis only half a mile behind them. She hadn't liked the taste of that beery old Stepmother, so she only snapped off her head and come on again.

'Drop your faggot across the path, little Dicky, and run for home!' says Jim.

So Black Annis bruised her legs and ran back to her cave to get an ointment to stop the bleeding. My mum says if a witch bleeds she loses all her power and dies.

And didn't Jim and Jen run too! But she wasn't scratched bad and back she come. She was only a quarter mile away when Jim looked, so they both dropped their faggots to trip her and ran for it.

Black Annis fell flat on her face over the firing but she caught up with them at their cottage door where their dad stood with an axe. And he threw it right in her face and her nose bled like a pig and she yelled and ran for her cave crying, 'Blood! Blood!' but the Christmas bells started pealing and she fell down far away and died.

Then the children kissed their dad and he'd brought a great load of firewood himself, and the stepmother was dead, and it was Christmas Eve so they made a big fire and had kippers and butter for tea. ('Butter?' said a rationed boy listener, 'Coo! what a feast!')

'It was Christmas Eve,' said the tale-teller firmly, 'and the old stepmother had been hiding all their rations to sell to the grocer's man so she could buy beer.'

('Did they find Black Annis? I asked.)

'The crows picked her bones – but one of my uncles he found a long tooth – ever so sharp it is – that's how I know it's quite true.'[17]

In Cromarty Firth Black Annis is called 'Gentle Annie' because of the treacherous wind that suddenly blows there on calm-seeming days.[18]

As time went on the heathen gods were increasingly regarded as demons, and the persecution of an animal is often a sign that it had once held the status of a god. The hunting of the wren can only be explained by postulating a time when it was sacred. In the North of Scotland a yellowhammer was persecuted as the Devil's bird who was said to drink a drop of the Devil's blood on May Day. The dark red scratches on the little greeny-blue egg were supposed to be a letter written to the Devil in the mother's blood, just as witches signed their compact with the Devil in their own blood. It seemed that the Devil had taken over the creatures that belonged to the sun god, for yellow came to be regarded as the Devil's special colour. Yellow irises are called 'the devil's flowers' in Newfoundland, and we have 'the primrose path to the everlasting bonfire'. Animals who were used much in magical cures and charms were probably once sacred, and cats have been unenviably distinguished in that way and have also been particularly associated with Satan. The cat, however, has a special distinction. Tradition has allotted to the cat tribe a king of its own. Both in the Celtic countries and in England there are tales of the King of the Cats. In the English version, which is particularly pleasing, it seems that the cat community, since the magnificent funerals of Ancient Egypt are no longer provided by humans, has managed to arrange that its king at least shall be buried with appropriate dignity.

The King of the Cats

A great many years ago there were two young men who were spending the Autumn on a shooting holiday up in the Highlands of Scotland. They were staying in a shooting lodge with an old woman to look after them; and her fine old black cat and their dogs were the only other company in the house. One day the elder of the two decided to stop at home, but the younger went out, to follow up some birds which he feared they had wounded the day before. So he set out in good time to follow the trail they had taken and to get back to supper before the early autumnal sunset. He did not come home until well after supper time, and his friend was beginning to get quite anxious about him when he came in, cold, wet and hungry. He muttered something about mist and sat down to supper, which he ate in silence. When it was finished and they were sitting by the fire smoking, with the cat sitting comfortably on the hearth-rug and the dogs lying down in the corner, he at length broke silence.

'I know you must be wondering what happened to me,' he said. 'I hardly know how to tell you, it was so strange. I followed on the track I meant to take and picked up a few birds, and it was well before sunset when I turned for home, but one of those mountain mists came down, and I got right off the track, and wandered round I don't know where until it was nearly dark. The dogs seemed as much puzzled as I was, and kept following trails here and there, until I saw a light in the distance and made for it. Just as I got up to it, it seemed to disappear, but I was just near a great old hollow oak, so I scrambled up it, thinking I might get a glimpse of the light from higher up. And as I climbed up I saw that the light was streaming up from the tree itself. So I scrambled up to look down into the hollow, and there I saw the most curious sight –'. He broke off: 'Just look at that cat! He's listening to me! I swear he understands every word I'm saying!' And sure enough, old Blackie was sitting straight up on the rug, looking with bright, excited eyes at the young man.

'Never mind the cat!' said his friend, knocking out his pipe. 'Tell me what you saw.'

'I seemed to be looking down into a church,' said the other. 'It was like a tiny cathedral, with lights and an altar, and in front of the altar was an open grave. Then I heard a mourning chant – a kind of howling and wauling sound, and outside below me the two dogs began to howl and scratch at the tree. The wailing came nearer and the funeral procession came into the church, but those bearing the coffin were all –' and the two young men looked down at the hearth-rug between them. 'Yes,' he went on, 'Cats. And on the coffin were laid a crown and a sceptre, and –' he broke off for old Blackie rose on his hind legs and shouted: 'By Jove! Old Peter's dead, and I'm King of the Cats!' With that he shot up the chimney and was never seen again.[19]

This story perceptively conveys the truth that the most domesticated of cats somehow contrives to lead an outside life of its own. 'Knurre-Murre', the Scandinavian version of the tale, does not include the episode of the funeral, and the speaking cat is accounted for by making him a troll in disguise.

In the Highland tradition the cat is not only provided with a king but with a god as well, Big Ears, a monstrous cat who was invoked in the barbarous ceremony, Taghairm. The last recorded celebration of Taghairm was in Mull in the seventeenth century and was described in the *London Literary Gazette* in March 1824. Particulars of it will be found in George Henderson's *Survivals in Belief Among the Celts* and in D. A. Mackenzie's *Scottish Folk-Lore and Folk Life*, as well as in several other books. Those who wish to have their feelings harrowed can read them there.[20]

In recent times the Irish have taken a very unfavourable view of cat nature. Lady Wilde paints a grim picture of them.

The Irish have always looked on cats as evil and mysteriously connected with some demoniacal influence. On entering a house the usual salutation is, 'God save all here except the cat'. Even the cake on the griddle may be blessed, but no-one says, 'God bless the cat'.

It is believed that the devil often assumes the form of these animals. The familiar of a witch is always a black cat; and it is supposed that black cats have powers and faculties quite different from all others of the feline tribe. They are endowed with reason, can understand conversations, and they are quite able to talk if they considered it advisable and judicious to join in the conversation. Their temperament is exceedingly unamiable, they are artful, malignant and skilled in deception, and people should be very cautious in caressing them, for they have the venomous heart and the evil eye, and are ever ready to do injury.[21]

It would perhaps be no wonder if the cats of Ireland, surrounded by such an atmosphere of distrust and a dislike amounting to hatred, should develop a hostile attitude towards mankind. Creatures as well as humans behave ill if ill is expected of them.

In Ireland, as well as in other parts of Britain, there is a King of the Cats, and, as might be expected, the King of the Cats is a particularly malevolent character. Lady Wilde writes:

A most important personage in feline history is the King of the Cats. He may be in your house, a common looking fellow enough, with no distinguishing mark of exalted rank about him, so that it is very difficult to verify his genuine claim to royalty. Therefore the best way is to cut off a tiny little bit of his ear. If he is really the royal personage, he will immediately speak out and declare who he is; and perhaps, at the same time, tell you some very disagreeable truths about yourself, not at all pleasant to have discussed by the house cat.

A man once, in a fit of passsion, cut off the head of the domestic pussy, and threw it on the fire. On which the head exclaimed in a fierce voice, 'Go tell your wife that you have cut off the head of the King of the Cats; but wait! I shall come back and be avenged for this insult,' and the eyes of the cat glared at him horribly from the fire.

And so it happened; for that day year, while the master of the house was playing with a pet kitten, it suddenly flew at his throat and bit him so severely that he died soon after.[22]

The transmigration of souls is a common feature in Irish folk tradition.

There seems some justification for the cat taking revenge here, and possibly the same might be said for Irusan, King of the Cats, who became involved in a conflict with Seanchan, the Chief Bard of Erin, and possibly the most disagreeable and cantankerous man in the whole land of Ireland.

It happened that when Seanchan was made Chief Bard of Ireland, King Guaire of Connaught gave a great feast of rich foods in his honour that lasted three days and three nights; all the bards of the country and all the nobles of Connaught attended it. But Seanchan fancied that the nobles were ranked equal with him and he refused all food, saying it was bad, and rejected all offers of service until at last a young girl persuaded him to accept the offer of an egg; but when she ran to fetch it the mice had eaten it. Then Seanchan made a terrible satire against the mice, so that ten of them fell down dead in his presence. 'It is well,' said Seanchan; 'but the cat is the one most to blame, for it was her duty to suppress the mice. Therefore I shall satirize the tribe of the cats, and their chief lord, Irusan, son of Arusan.'

And he said – 'Irusan, monster of claws, who strikes at the mouse, but lets it go; weakest of cats. The otter did well who bit off the tips of thy progenitor's ears, so that every cat since is jagged-eared. Let thy tail hang down; it is right, for the mouse jeers at them.'

When Irusan heard the satire he promised vengeance on

Seanchan, but his daughter, Sharp-tooth, said, 'Bring him here alive that we may all take vengeance on him.'

So Irusan set out to fetch him from Guaire's court, and when Seanchan heard that Irusan was on his way to kill him he was frightened, and begged for protection from King Guaire, and all the nobles stood by to protect him. The narrative goes on:

> And before long a vibrating, impressive, impetuous sound was heard, like a raging tempest of fire in full blaze. And when the cat appeared he seemed to them of the size of a bullock; and this was his appearance – rapacious, panting, jagged-eared, snub-nosed, sharp-toothed, nimble, angry, vindictive, glare-eyed, terrible, sharp-clawed. Such was his similitude. But he passed on amongst them, not minding till he came to Seanchan; and him he seized by the arm and jerked him up on his back, and made off the way he came before any one could touch him; for he had no other object in view but to get hold of the poet.

Seanchan, who does not come well out of this adventure, tried to mollify the cat with flattery, but Irusan kept his mouth firmly closed, and bore the bard on towards his cave. Things would have gone ill indeed with Seanchan if they had not passed St Kieran's forge at Clonmacnoise, with the Saint himself standing at the door.

'"What!" exclaimed the saint; "is that the Chief Bard of Erin on the back of a cat? Has Guaire's hospitality ended in this?" And he ran for a red-hot bar of iron that was in the furnace, and struck the cat on the side with it, so that he fell down lifeless.'

That was the end of poor Irusan, but Seanchan had learned nothing from experience, for as soon as he was on his feet he cursed the Saint for interfering, for if he had been killed Guaire's lack of hospitality would have been blamed for it. In fact, Seanchan ended, the whole affair was Guaire's fault. After this all the kings were very careful not to offend Seanchan, and he was treated with anxious consideration.[23]

In another of Lady Wilde's stories the cat was the aggressor. It was indeed a demon rather than a cat.

There was a woman in Connemara, the wife of a fisherman,

and as he always had very good luck, she had plenty of fish at all times stored away in the house ready for market. But to her great annoyance she found that a great cat used to come in at night and devour all the best and finest fish. So she kept a big stick by her and determined to watch.

One day, as she and a woman were spinning together, the house suddenly became quite dark; and the door was burst open as if by the blast of the tempest, when in walked a huge black cat, who went straight up to the fire, then turned round and growled at them.

'Why, surely this is the devil!' said a young girl, who was by, sorting the fish.

'I'll teach you how to call me names,' said the cat; and, jumping at her, he scratched her arm till the blood came. 'There now,' he said, 'you will be more civil another time when a gentleman comes to see you.' And with that he walked over to the door and shut it close to prevent any of them going out, for the poor young girl, while crying loudly from fright and pain, had made a desperate rush to get away.

Just then a man was going by, and hearing the cries he pushed open the door and tried to get in, but the cat stood on the threshold and would let no one pass. On this, the man attacked him with his stick, and gave him a sound blow; the cat, however, was more than his match in the fight, for it flew at him and tore his face and hands so badly that the man at last took to his heels and ran away as fast as he could.

'Now it's time for my dinner,' said the cat, going up to examine the fish that was laid out on the tables. 'I hope the fish is good to-day. Now don't disturb me, nor make a fuss; I can help myself.' With that he jumped up and began to devour all the best fish, while he growled at the woman.

'Away, out of this, you wicked beast!' she cried, giving it a blow with the tongs that would have broken his back, only it was a devil; 'out of this! No fish shall you have to-day.'

But the cat only grinned at her, and went on tearing and spoiling and devouring the fish, evidently not a bit the worse for the blow. On this, both the women attacked it with sticks, and struck hard blows enough to kill it, on which the cat glared at them, and spit fire; then making a leap, it tore their hands and arms till the blood came, and the frightened women rushed shrieking from the house.

But presently the mistress returned, carrying with her a bottle of holy water; and looking in, she saw the cat still devouring the fish, and not minding. So she crept over quietly and threw the holy water on it without a word. No sooner was this done than a dense black smoke filled the place, through which nothing was seen but the two red eyes of the cat, burning like coals of fire. Then the smoke gradually cleared away, and she saw the body of the creature burning slowly, till it became shrivelled and black like a cinder, and finally disappeared. And from that time the fish remained untouched and safe from harm, for the power of the Evil One was broken, and the demon cat was seen no more.[24]

Lady Wilde has little good to say of cats except for praise of their beauty and elegant, well-bred ways, and of their wise training of their kittens. But she gives us one tale of a cat, evidently a close friend of the fairies, whom even she admires for her charming manners and kindly dealings. She says:

A story is current also, that one night an old woman was sitting up very late spinning when a knocking came to the door. 'Who's there?' she asked. No answer; but still the knocking went on. 'Who is there?' she asked a second time. No answer; and the knocking continued.

'Who is there?' she asked the third time in a very angry passion.

Then there came a small voice – 'Ah, Judy, agrah, let me in, for I am cold and hungry; open the door, Judy, agrah, and let me sit by the fire, for the night is cold out there. Judy, agrah, let me in, let me in!'

The heart of Judy was touched, for she thought it was some small child that had lost its way, and she rose up from her spinning, and went and opened the door – when in walked a large black cat with a white breast, and two white kittens after her.

They all made over to the fire and began to warm and dry

themselves, purring all the time very loudly; but Judy said never a word, only went on spinning.

Then the black cat spoke at last – 'Judy, agrah, don't stay up so late again, for the fairies wanted to hold a council here to-night, and to have some supper, but you have prevented them; so they were very angry and determined to kill you, and only for myself and my two daughters here you would be dead by this time. So take my advice, don't interfere with the fairy hours again, for the night is theirs, and they hate to look on the face of a mortal when they are out for pleasure or business. So I ran on to tell you, and now give me a drink of milk, for I must be off.'

And after the milk was finished the cat stood up, and called her daughters to come away.

'Good-night, Judy, agrah,' she said. 'You have been very civil to me, and I'll not forget it to you, Good night, good night.'

With that the black cat and the two kittens whisked up the chimney; but Judy looking down saw something glittering on the hearth, and taking it up she found it was a piece of silver, more than she could ever make in a month by her spinning, and she was glad in her heart, and never again sat up so late to interfere with the fairy hours, but the black cat and her daughters came no more to the house.[25]

Where could one find a more kindly, considerate animal? Whatever Lady Wilde's general opinion of cats she dealt with them fairly in this tale.

One may guess that old Judy was kind to all cats after that night, in memory of the three who had turned aside the fatal ill-will of the fairies.

2 Feline Characteristics

The cat is almost as much the subject of proverbs and proverbial phrases as the dog. 'A cat has nine lives', 'Curiosity killed the cat', 'As melancholy as a gib-cat', 'A lucky black cat', 'To make a cat's paw of him', 'To play cat and mouse', are popular phrases that spring to mind, and a good many nursery rhymes deal with cats in a lively and creative way.

> Diddlety, diddlety dumpty;
> The cat ran up the plum tree.
> Half a crown
> To fetch her down;
> Diddlety, diddlety dumpty.[1]

or

> As I was going to St Ives,
> I met a man with seven wives;
> Each wife had seven sacks,
> Each sack had seven cats,
> Each cat had seven kits:
> Kits, cats, sacks, wives,
> How many were going to St Ives?[2]

'Pussy Cat, Pussy Cat, where have you been?',[3] 'Ding-dong bell',[4] 'The Craws hae killed the pussy O'[5] and about a dozen more.

19

Already by medieval times the cat is a traditional part of the domestic scene. We find a pleasing description of it in that medieval best-seller, *De Proprietate Rerum*, compiled by Bartholomew Anglicus, a thirteenth-century Franciscan friar. It was translated into English at the end of the same century by Trevisa, and into French, Spanish and Dutch by the end of the fourteenth. It draws on earlier books from the second century or so, but the description of a domestic cat has the air of being taken from direct observation.

He is a full lecherous beast in youth, swift, pliant, and merry, and leapeth and reseth on everything that is to fore him; and is led by a straw, and playeth therewith: and is a right heavy beast in age and full sleepy, and lieth slyly in wait for mice: and is aware where they be more by smell than by sight, and hunteth and reseth on them in privy places: and when he taketh a mouse, he playeth therewith, and eateth him after the play. In time of love is hard fighting for wives, and one scratcheth and rendeth the other grievously with biting and with claws. And he maketh a ruthful noise and ghastful, when one proffereth to fight with another; and unneth is hurt when he is thrown down off an high place.[6]

An even longer and fuller description of the cat is given by Edward Topsell in his *Historie of Four-Footed Beastes* (1607). A good many beliefs and traditions about cats are told in the course of it, with strange remedies and traditional medical beliefs interspersed among them. The cat's voice and actions are vividly described.

It is needelesse to spende any time about her loving nature to man, how she flattereth by rubbing her skinne against ones Legges, how she whurleth with her voyce, having as many runes as turnes, for she hath one voice to beg and to complain, another to testifie her delight and pleasure, another among hir own kind by flattring, by hissing, by puffing, by spitting, insomuch as some have thought that they have a peculiar intelligible language among themselves. Therefore how she beggeth, playeth, leapeth, catcheth, tosseth with her foote, riseth up to strings held over her head, sometime creeping, sometimes lying on the back, playing with one foot, sometime on the bely, snatching, now with mouth, and anone with foot, aprenending greedily anything save the hand of a man with divers such gestical actions, it is needelesse to stand upon; insomuch as *Coelius* was wont to say, that being free from his Studies and more urgent waighty affaires, he was not ashamed to play and sport himselfe, with his Cat, and verily it may well be called an idle mans pastime.[7]

Topsell goes on to warn his readers against caressing cats too lovingly, for they carry poison and infection in their breath, and people who sleep with them and love them too fondly are likely to be infected with consumption or hectic fevers. He also tells of men who suffer from an allergy to cats, a peculiarity which is still not uncommon.

There are many folktales and legends which comment on special aspects of feline characteristics. Ruth Tongue has collected one Somerset legend, about Tarr Steps, which might be a gloss upon the well-known proverb 'Curiosity killed the cat'. It is hardly favourable to the cat's character, but we are not expressly told that all cats are like this.

The Curious Cat

There were once a curious cat over to Spire, a proper mischievous nuisance that cat were, always poking into anything new. He'd torment they pore liddle mice and birds shocking – just to see what they'd try to do. 'Twere a wonder he didn't get his whiskers scythed off in hay field and his tail broke to bits on dreshen-floor for he were always right in the way where nobody wanted 'n. But there, he'd bite and scratch and swear till every one wished him Somewhere Else.

One day he went for a walk and he found Mouncey Castle. 'Now, who dropped this little lot?' say he. 'I must go and see.' Then in the woodside he come on a gurt stone, twelve foot or more, just dropped there, and he knew he were getting nearer. Then he heard yells of rage and off he scuttles to see what 'twas and it were the Devil and Parson, one on each side of the Barle and a new stone bridge atwen 'n. 'I'll have a look-see at that,' says Cat and downhill he goes.

Says Parson to Devil, 'You shan't have none of my souls be first step on your bridge. They bain't goin' Somewhere Else.'

'You old black crow,' yells Devil.

'If I be a crow,' says Parson, 'I bain't so black as yew!'

And just then puss walk out over onto Tarr Steps to look it over, no matter if he'd been invited or no. The Devil pounced on 'n like a lightning flash – and poor Cat goed Somewhere Else quicker than you could think![8]

This is a rather pleasing version of the tale of 'The Devil's Bridge', in which there is at least some vestige of justice about the victim's fate. Generally it is a dog, who innocently follows a piece of meat thrown over to entice him. Actually the stone bridge is a set of natural stepping stones across the river Barle, and Mouncey Castle is an earthwork near at hand, apparently supposed to be the Devil's workmanship.

There is another Somerset tale of cats' curiosity told by Ruth Tongue in *Folktales of England*, but in this the little cat was frightened away from a dangerous investigation by a kindly tree spirit, The Apple-Tree Man, who was traditionally supposed to live in the oldest tree in the orchard.

Tibb's Cat and the Apple-Tree Man

There was a little cat down Tibb's Farm, not much more'n a kitten – a little dairy-maid with a face so clean as a daisy. A pretty little dear her was, but her wanted to know too much. There was fields down along as wasn't liked. No one cared much about working there. Y'see, 'twas all elder there, and there was a queer wind used to blow there most times, and sound like someone talking it would. I wouldn't go there myself unless I had a criss-cross of salt on a crust. Oh! yes, my maid, I could show'ee the field now, but I 'on't, and don't you be like Tibb's cat, and go look-see for yourself! There's summat bad about down there, and that was why all they wild black cats goed there on certain nights, and Tibb's cat she wished to go too. She tried to find the way Candle-mas Eve, and Allern (Hallowe'en) and all the wisht nights witches do meet, but her weren't big enough to catch up. So, when New Year's Eve come, she tried again.

This time she got as far as the orchet, and then the Apple-Tree Man he called out to her, 'Yew go on back whoame, my dear. There's folk a-coming to pour cider for my roots, and shoot off guns to drive away the witches. This be no place for yew. Yew go back whoame, and don't come a-wandering round at night till St. Tibb's Eve.'

The little dairy-maid her took off home with her tail stiff with vright. Properly scared she, the Apple-Tree Man did. And she never wandered at night again, 'cause she didn't know when St. Tibb's Eve is. Nor do anybody else.[9]

A 'dairy-maid' is a white and tortoise-shell cat. Ruth Tongue cites a saying from Pitminster – 'You want to know too much, like Tibb's Cat.'

There are many tales and stories told to illustrate the cat's astuteness and presence of mind, from the story of Puss-in-Boots to short origin legends, as, for instance, the legend of 'The Cat's Allotment' to be found in *Folktales of Israel*, whose source is in Libya. At the beginning of the world, when each animal was allotted its source of food the Almighty asked the cat if he would choose his daily food from a shop-keeper, a peasant or a farmer, but the cat preferred to make a more explicit choice. He replied without hesitation 'Give me my daily bread from an absent-minded woman who leaves the kitchen door open.' He does not always attain to this happiness but it has remained his ideal ever since.[10]

In *Old Peter's Russian Tales*, Arthur Ransome retells a Russian Nursery Tale, 'The Cat who became Head-Forester' which paints a picture of the cat's intelligence, self-assumption and his quiet assurance that he is made to be waited upon and fed by others with a minimum of exertion on his own account. It is the story of a tough old Tom, scarred with a hundred battles with one ear missing, master of the village cats. He lived with an old peasant who was heartily sick of his bellicose ways and determined to get rid of him and get a pretty, placid little cat in his place. But it is no easy matter to get rid of a cat, which is the hardest thing in the world to kill, and as to losing it, no bad penny ever turned up more persistently than a cat who wants to come home. So at last the peasant bundled Old Tom into a sack, sewed it up securely, and then trudged into the heart of the forest carrying it on his back. When he was miles from home he twirled the sack round, flung it as far away as he could and went back home to buy a pretty, placid young cat for a few twists of tobacco. He never gave another thought to poor old Tom in his sack, and as a matter of fact he didn't need to. Old Tom was frightened enough when he found himself twirling through the air, but he managed to fall on his feet, bag or no bag, and after panting a little he began to claw a hole in the bag, and soon got one paw out, and then another, and then his head, and presently he was clear of the whole thing and started to explore the forest. After a time he found a little empty hut which had once belonged to one of the foresters, and he settled down comfortably for the night. In the morning he set to work to hunt birds and mice, and found it quite an easy job, but it seemed to him beneath his dignity to hunt for food; he was accustomed to being fed. So he began to look around to find someone to attend on him. It happened that by good fortune he met a pretty little fox, a maiden fox, who was much struck with this war-scarred veteran with only one ear. She approached him with distinguished politeness and enquired his name. 'Don't you know,' he said haughtily, 'That I am Cat Ivanovitch, who has been sent down from the Siberian Forests to be Head Forester of these regions?' The little fox, Lisabetta Ivanovna, was tremendously impressed.

She led Cat Ivanovitch to her neat, warm earth, and gave him a most delicious meal of game. And while they were both full of good cheer she shyly suggested that they should get married, to which Cat Ivanovitch consented. The little fox cooked up all the delicacies she had in the house and they had a splendid wedding, after which Cat Ivanovitch curled up in the most comfortable place and went to sleep, while Lisabetta went out to hunt for food. She had not to go far before she met Michael Wolf and Levan the Bear, and she impressed them both so much with the prowess of her husband that they hurried into the forest to fetch him a sheep and a bull. And so it went on, and Cat Ivanovitch and Lisabetta Ivanovna had nothing to do all the rest of their lives but to accept the good fare that was brought for them and to amuse themselves occasionally with a little hunting for sport.[11]

One of the *Folktales of Hungary*, edited by Linda Dégh, is on the same kind of plot, but the prestige of the hero is not so much founded on bragging as on bellicose performance. It is the tale of 'Cecus-Becus Berneusz'.

A man who had two cats took one to market to sell it, and the new owner enquired how it ought to be fed. 'Oh, whatever you want to give it will do', said its old master.

The new owner interpreted this very liberally, for when he got home he had one of his oxen killed and fed the cat on the meat. This set the pattern. In a year the cat was enormous, and had eaten up almost everything his master possessed, and the poor man had no idea how to get rid of it. He went to a neighbour for advice, who could think of nothing better than to burn down his house after they had locked the cat inside. But when the flames grew high around him the cat escaped through the smoke-hole.

Then the neighbours advised that he should ride with the cat to the deepest part of the forest, kill his horse and leave Cecus Becus to eat the carcase. This lasted Cecus Becus Berneusz for a long time, and before it was finished a fox arrived and wanted to take his share. But the cat dashed out from behind the carcase so that the fox ran off in a fright, leaving some of his fur behind on the cat's claws. It ran and ran until it ran into a wolf.

'What's the matter, Brother Fox?' said the wolf.

'Oh, the terrible Cecus Becus Berneusz has given me such a fright that I can't stop running. Go and see him, and kill him if you can.'

'Oh, I'll kill him quick enough,' said the wolf. But when he got to the dead horse Cecus Becus launched himself at him like a thunderbolt, and he turned tail and ran, and ran straight back to where the fox was waiting. They went on together and met one by one a tiger, a wild boar and a bear, and each of them went to

destroy the terrible Cecus Becus Berneusz, and everyone was put
to flight. So they got together and they decided to give a banquet
to the gallant Cecus Becus Berneusz. They got the feast ready but
there was some discussion as to which should take the invitation,
however in the end the wolf went, and the gallant Cecus Becus
Berneusz paced in a stately way behind him. The feast was all
spread out under a greaty lofty tree. 'Now,' mumbled the bear,
'Here he comes. We're five to one. Let's fall on him all at once and
tear him to pieces.'

But Cecus Becus felt the danger prickling in his whiskers. He
burst through the little cluster of his hosts, and shot up the tree; up
and up to the very top. The animals were furious. Only one of
them could climb, but they piled up on top of each other and tried
to reach him. The wolf was on top. When he got near, Cecus
Becus sneezed; a monstrous sneeze so that Wolf lost his balance
and fell right to the bottom and was killed. The others tried to
scramble down and clawed at each other and fell. Some broke
their necks and some their legs. Cecus Becus sat there for a time
and then climbed down and went home. He led his master to the
spot with a big hand-cart and they gathered up enough meat to
last them for a long time. This is the nearest we get in folk

tradition to a representation of the large part which territorial rights play in cats' sociology.[12]

Some folktales, however, throw a more favourable light upon the cat's character. The Irish estimate of a cat is not usually a high one, but in Sean O'Sullivan's *Folktales of Ireland* there is a rather touching anecdote of the cat's dogged devotion to his duty in the business of catching rats and mice, in the story 'The Big Cat and the Big Rat'.

There was once a man in Galway who was plagued almost to death by a monstrous big rat. Every morning when he came in from his early work and sat down to his breakfast, this great creature, bigger than any rat that anyone had ever seen, came in at the door, jumped on to the table and began to devour the breakfast set out for the poor man of the house, and she looked so terrible and fierce that no one dared to lift a hand against her. This went on day after day until the poor man was sure she would destroy them all with hunger. So he thought he would go and buy a good strong cat. So he bought one, a nine-months-old cat, big and strong. The man brought him in and told his wife to give him a

good feed of milk. She did so, and the cat licked himself and settled down by the fire. When the man came in for his breakfast next morning the rat came in as usual, and the cat got up and made for the rat. The rat sidled up to it, and a terrible fight began. But they hadn't been fighting long when the cat began to mew piteously, for the rat was fairly tearing him to pieces. It went on at him for another quarter of an hour till the poor cat's courage broke and he dashed away and hid in a corner of the room. Then the rat jumped up on to the table and she ate all she wanted of the man's breakfast, and then went calmly away. The poor cat crept up to the fire, all torn and bleeding, and his mistress brought him a good bowl of milk, and he drank it and licked his wounds, and mewed at the door. He looked left and right out of it, and went cautiously away. He did not come back again that day, nor the next, nor the next, but on the fourth day, early in the morning, there was a mew outside the door, and there stood the biggest cat they had ever seen, or would ever see again, and their own little cat beside it. They walked up to the fire, and they both mewed. 'Give them a quart of milk!' said the master of the house, and his heart lifted with hope. They both drank till it was finished, and the big cat lay down on the hearth while the little cat jumped upon a chair. The master of the house sat down to his breakfast, the door opened and the big rat came in. As soon as the big cat saw her he got up and twirled his tail, but the small cat ran away in terror. Then the rat sidled up to the big cat, and the fight began. There never was such clawing and tearing and biting before. They fought round and round the kitchen all the morning and half the afternoon. Then out they went into the yard and went three great courses round it, and as the sun was setting, the great cat killed the monstrous rat, and there was an end to it. Then the great cat, torn and bleeding, dragged himself up to the fire, and the little cat followed him. They both put up their heads and mewed for milk, and you may be sure the lady of the house ran to get them as much as they wanted. Then they rested by the fire and licked themselves. After a while the big cat went to the door and mewed, and the little one followed, and neither of them were seen in those parts again.[13]

Enid Porter has an anecdote in *The Folklore of East Anglia* of a man called Jabez Few of Willingham who kept some white rats which were supposed by the neighbours to be devil's imps – as I imagine the monster rat was – and he put one of them in a woman's bedroom as a prank. A large ginger cat was shut into the room to deal with it. There was a tremendous racket and at length they opened the door and found the room full of loose fur and the cat rushing up and down the bed-curtains like a mad thing. But the rat was still uncaptured. The owner of the house was about to resort to magic and was threatening to shoot Jabez Few besides, when Jabez came into the house and whistled, and the white rat ran out and went to him quite meekly. This happened some time in the 1920s, but there was no magical cat to come to the rescue.[14]

So far we have heard about cats in their relationship to human beings and their conflicts with other creatures, but tradition has had little to tell us about their social lives among themselves, their love affairs, their concerts or their rivalries. There are, however, a few folktales which touch on these subjects. In Andrew Lang's *Pink Fairy Book* there appears at two removes a Japanese cat romance translated from *Japanische Märchen und Sagen* by David Braune. It is 'The Cat's Elopement'.

There was once a very beautiful cat called Gon, with fur as smooth and shining as silk and the most beautiful green eyes, who belonged to a music teacher, who loved him dearly for his sweet and engaging ways, and would not have parted with him for the world.

Not far away there lived a most beautiful little cat, with soft fur and a nose like marzipan and large, loving eyes. She was called Koma, and her mistress doted on her as much as Gon's master did on him. One night, when each of them had gone out for a walk, it happened that they met, and fell at once deeply in love with each other. They wanted to spend their whole lives together, and could not bear to meet only for snatched moments. When they had consulted together, long and earnestly, Gon went to his master and begged him to allow him to go and live with Koma, but his master would not think for a moment of parting with him. Then Koma went to her mistress and begged that she might be allowed to live with her dear husband, but this seemed even less possible, and their owners were so afraid of losing them that they kept them almost as prisoners and it was difficult for them to see each other at all, and they at length sadly decided that they must leave their kind master and mistress and go out into the wide world. It is as easy to hold quicksilver between your finger and thumb as to keep a cat who means to escape; so one dark night they both slipped away and went into the wide world together. They went on, day after day, finding food as best they could; out of their home town and through the flowery country until they came to the great Imperial City. They went through the crowded, busy streets until they found a beautiful great park. It was the garden of the Imperial Palace, though they did not know it. They felt that this was a place to live, and they were licking each other tenderly under a flowering tree when they heard a terrible barking and growling and a great mastiff rushed up to attack them. Koma shot up the tree, but Gon turned to defend her. He would have had but little chance against the great mastiff, but Koma lifted up her voice and cried aloud for help. One of the Palace attendants ran up with a stick and drove the dog away. He saw what a beautiful cat Gon was and took him away in his arms to present him to the Princess, who lived in a palace of her own in the grounds. The Princess was delighted with Gon and with his pretty ways and could hardly bear him out of her sight; but where was Koma? In any moment that he could get away Gon searched about, and asked for news of her, but he could discover nothing, and could only wait and try to hope.

The Princess had her troubles too, for she was persecuted by the attentions of a serpent which had fallen in love with her, a sinister and dangerous suitor. Her maids had orders to prevent his entry, but he was subtle, and the maids were sometimes careless. One day she was sitting on her cushions playing upon her zither when she felt something gliding up her sash. It was the snake, who had found his way in, and was sliding up her body to kiss her cheek. She screamed and threw herself backward. Gon was asleep on a cushion by her side. In a moment he was up and had seized the serpent by the neck. A nip and a shake, and he laid it dead on the matting beside her, never to trouble her again. The Princess picked Gon up and kissed and praised him. After this nothing was too good for him. The best tit-bits and the softest mats were his, and if only he could find his Koma he felt that he had nothing to wish for.

One day, as he was lying by the window looking out he saw a

great hulking Tom Cat bullying and tormenting a little Tib. Full of rage he leapt out of the window and went to the rescue. He hurled himself against the bully and put him to flight at once. Then he turned to comfort the little lady cat and could hardly believe his eyes when he saw that it was his own Koma. The two purred and rubbed themselves against each other, almost frantic with joy. Then Gon led his little wife proudly to the Palace and together they told the Princess all their story. She wept with pity for them, and promised that they should never be separated again.

Before very long the Princess married a Prince, who came to live with her in the Palace, and the Princess told him how Gon had saved her from the snake and of the sorrows the two lovers had had, and he valued them as she did, and promised they should always stay with the Princess. And Koma and Gon had many children, and so did the Prince and Princess, and they played together happily as long as they lived.[15]

The Magic Orange Tree, a collection newly published of some Haitian folktales, gives us a very lively parody on the cats' concert, not always welcome to human beings, and the bellicose exercises that sometimes follow it.

The Cat's Baptism

It was time for the smallest cat's baptism. Mr. and Mrs. Cat spoke with the child's godfather. They spoke with their relatives, and they spoke with the priest. The baptism was arranged for the following Sunday.

The Cat family, in their finest clothes, walked solemnly and proudly to the church. They sat in the front rows, attentive and eager. When the priest, a large brown cat, stepped onto the pulpit, the service began.

The priest sang:
Meow meow meow
meow meow.
All the members of the church responded.
Meow meow meow
meow meow.
The priest continued to chant:
Meow meow meow
meow meow.

And the congregation responded:

Meow meow meow

meow meow.

Then the priest held up his hand for silence and motioned to the godfather to step forward. 'Please,' the priest said, 'kindly sing the prayers for your godchild.'

The godfather sang:

Meow

'I beg your pardon,' the priest said. 'I do not understand you. What was that?'

The godfather sang again:

Meow

'What?' the priest cried. 'You are not singing properly at all. Sing after me.

Meow meow meow

meow meow.'

The godfather sang:

Meow

'You are insulting the priest!' one of the cats from the other side of the church cried out, and he ran over and smacked the godfather. YAOH! Two members of the Cat family rushed up and smacked him. YAOH! Meow! PAAA! One of the cats had bitten the tail of the priest, thinking he was the godfather. Five more cats joined the fight and soon all the cats in the church were fighting.

Meow meow meow MEOW MEOW meow meow meow MEOW meow meow meow meow MEOW meow MEOW meow meow MEOW meow MEOW meow meow MEOW meow meow meow MEOW . . . . . . meow.[16]

3
Traditional Enemies

In the folklore of cats there are two sets of traditional enemies. The dog is the enemy of the cat and the cat is the enemy of the mouse. There are many myths and legends told to account for this enmity. The domestic position which they hold partly accounts for it. To be forced into close proximity with different tastes, habits and rewards is to be in a position of perpetual competition, and this is often the explanation given of their mutual hostility. In the traditional old-fashioned working household the domestic animals are valued not for themselves but for the performance of the work allotted to them. The dog's work is done out of doors; he guards the house, chases game and kills rats in the granary. His home is in the yard and the fields. The cat kills mice and keeps those rats in check which venture inside the house. His home is indoors, his resting place is by the fire. Though he does live indoors he is less confined than a dog, for he can climb vertical walls, and find his way out of every open window and smoke-vent.

The dog works as a rule with the men. He is a pack animal, and regards the pack-leader with natural veneration. The cat's unit is a small family group; he has not the same natural organ of veneration as a dog. He works under the guidance of women and since he is a taut animal, hunting always under great nervous strain, he appreciates gentleness, smooth caresses and quiet voices. The different natures of the animals seem to have directed their specializations, but mankind is a story-telling creature and a natural scientist, always eager to know the reason for everything, and it is natural that various legends should be told to account for the relationship between the two household domestic animals, each at once the servant and the pet of mankind.

In most of the stories the dog and cat are friends at first, until a cause of dissension arises between them. One which is little known but quite representative is to be found in *New Tales from Grimm*, known from childhood by Ruth Michaelis-Jena and translated and edited by her and her husband, Arthur Ratcliff. It is called 'Why Dogs Dislike Cats and Cats Dislike Mice'. It seems to be an offshoot from the early cycle of animal stories, generally called *Reynard the Fox*.

A dog had served a lion faithfully for many years and so the King of the Animals wished to honour his faithful servant. One day he said to the dog, 'Hearken to me; from this day onwards you shall be one of my nobles!' And he gave him a patent of nobility, drawn up on parchment in handsome lettering all decorated with gold.

The faithful dog was delighted, and went off to the cat, his great friend, and said,

> 'Good cousin, the King has conferred a high honour on me. To this end he has given me a parchment in handsome letter-ing all decorated with gold. Will you be good enough to store that parchment for me, and keep a sharp eye on it to see it doesn't get damaged or stolen, till the day I come back and fetch it.'

The cat, promising to do so, hid the parchment down a hole in a great oak-tree, where it seemed quite safe. To satisfy the dog, the cat at first kept regular watch over it, to make sure it did not get damaged by rain, but in time she forgot to do so any more.

Meanwhile, a hungry little mouse, happening to come across the parchment, nibbled at it every day till at length it was all tattered and torn.

At last the dog came to the cat and asked for his parchment, as he had to take it with him to a tournament at the royal court. So the cat discovered the ruin wrought in the hollow tree by the mouse. Furious at what had happened, the cat swore everlasting war on the mouse, and the dog likewise on the cat. And from that time on they have never been able to bear each other.[1]

These archetypal animals never seem to be able to forgive and forget, but carry their feuds on for countless generations.

There are several of these origin stories in which the dog and cat are already domestic animals, but co-operate with each other in the service of the humans until some situation arises which brings them in opposition to each other. It is nearly always the cat who shows wisdom and resource in these circumstances and the dog who acts foolishly, though sometimes rivalry springs up between them and they became irreconcilable enemies.

A story of the first type is to be found in *Folk-Tales from Korea* collected by Professor Zong-in-Sob. It was told him by Zong-Dog-Zoh of Oyang in 1915.

It is the tale of a very poor old couple, a fisherman and his wife, who lived in a tiny cottage with a dog and cat to whom they were devoted. The old fisherman went out on the sea every day and caught fish which his wife sold in the market, so that they gained a precarious livelihood.

One day the old man went out to his fishing, and fished all day without having a single bite. He decided in the end that he might as well give it up, but he made one last cast and felt a heavy fish on his line. It was a great carp. As he drew it out of the water it looked at him very sadly, and he was sure that it had tears in its eyes. It curved its body round and looked longingly at the sea, as if it was begging him to let it go. He was convinced that it was a sacred fish, and at once he took it gently off the hook and put it into the sea. It swam away, but before it disappeared under the waves it turned and looked back once and twice with deep gratitude. He went home empty-handed, but sure that he had done the right thing.

Next day he went back to the same place to fish, and as he was casting in his line a young boy appeared before him in a wide straw hat and saluted him with both hands, most respectfully. 'The Dragon King has sent me to invite you to his palace at the

bottom of the sea. He is deeply grateful to you for saving the life of his son, the Prince, yesterday. Follow me.' He turned round facing the sea and murmured an incantation. At once a broad, dry way appeared, leading down to the bottom of the sea. The boy led the way and the old fisherman followed. They went down and down into the heart of the sea. At length they reached a magnificent palace with richly dressed attendants standing at the gates, and entered the royal park. On and on they went past noble buildings, until they reached one finer than all the rest, and at the door of it stood a splendid figure, the Dragon King. He came forward and greeted the old man with a deep obeisance. 'I have longed to see you,' he said, 'to thank you for sparing the life of my dear son, my heir. Come into the palace and be our guest, and we will do all in our power to make you happy.' And he led the old fisherman into the palace. There were all delights there, of music and feasting and songs, and the old man was as happy as the day was long, except that as time passed he grew increasingly anxious about his old wife, dying perhaps of hunger and pining for the loss of him. At length he went to the Dragon King, and begged to be allowed to go home to his wife. The King was very reluctant to let him go, but at length he told him that he might leave next day. That night the Prince, who was always very friendly with him, came to him and said: 'Tomorrow the King, my father, will ask you to choose a present to take with you. You should choose the iron measure that stands in the jewel-box beside the throne. It is the most precious thing in the kingdom, for it will give you whatever you ask for.' So the next day when the King bade the old fisherman a kind farewell, he invited him to choose anything he would like out of the kingdom and the fisherman said that best

36

of all he would like the old iron measure. 'I am sorry,' said the King, 'that is the only thing that you cannot have.' The Prince was standing beside the throne, and he said: 'My father, give him what he asks. After all, he has saved my life. Would you rather have me or the measure?' At that the Dragon King gave the old man the measure, and said to him kindly 'Good fortune go with you, my friend, wherever you may go.'

The fisherman was taken home, where his wife and the cat and the dog were beside themselves with joy to see him. He led them all out of the cottage and he asked the measure to take down the old cottage and put a fine house in its place. And in a twinkling it was done. The old woman was amazed, but her husband warned her to keep the measure safely hidden and to tell no one of its powers, for it would give them whatever they asked. 'Then let me ask for food,' said the old woman, who was very hungry, and at once it was full of rice. 'Let us keep it always full of rice,' she said, and from that day the measure was never empty. What the pair did not need for food they sold, and soon became quite rich. Their neighbours of course noticed the change in their condition and the fine new house which had suddenly appeared, and there was much gossip about it.

One day a covetous and dishonest woman, a shopkeeper who lived near the river, called at the house while the old man was out in his boat. She brought with her some jewels which she offered for sale, or exchange for rice, and approached the old woman with flattering congratulations on her good fortune.

'For, of course,' she said, 'we all know that you have a magic measure that is always full of rice. There are no secrets in this world. As the old proverb says: "Rats listen to what you say at night and birds in the daytime." How dear you must be to the gods to possess such a wonderful measure! Let me show you my jewels. Surely your attire should match your fortune.'

She spread out the jewels, and the old woman was flattered and tempted. She went to fetch the measure from its secret place, chose one of the jewels and gave the shopkeeper as much rice as she wanted for it. That night as the old couple were asleep, the house was broken open and the measure was stolen from its secret hiding place. When they looked for it in the morning it was gone. The old woman at once suspected the shopkeeper, and confessed to her husband that she had let the woman see the measure. He was angry, but they could think of no way of proving that she was the thief. From that day they grew gradually poorer and poorer and soon they had hardly enough food to feed the cat and dog. The two animals were much grieved at the misfortune which had happened to their people, and determined to try what they could to get the magic measure back. They watched the shopkeeper carefully, and one night they saw her come out of her house and swim across the river. They followed her a long way up into the hills until she came to a large house. It belonged to a kinsman of hers, well known as a desperate robber. They waited outside, and she came back with a big measure of rice. They were sure then that the measure was hidden there. They determined to get it back. Night after night they visited the thief's house in the mountains, and often they saw the woman going there and coming back with rice, but they did not know where the measure was hidden. One night they saw the thief himself coming out of the house and going to a big storehouse in the garden. He came out with a big measure of rice, locked the door of the storehouse and went into his house. They were sure the measure was there.

The dog waited in the garden and the cat went hunting until he caught a rat. He seized it, and said: 'Take me at once to your King, as you value your life.' The rat led him to where the King of the

Rats was sitting, and the cat at once leapt on him and seized him inexorably. 'As you value your life,' it said, 'tell me if there is an iron measure in that place which holds an endless store of rice.' 'It is there,' said the Rat King. 'Where is it hidden?' said the cat. 'It is inside a stone chest which is locked. We cannot reach it', said the Rat King. 'You will reach it before tomorrow morning,' said the cat, 'or you will die the death.' Then all the loyal rat people promised to do all they could to open the chest. They formed two great armies, under General Awltoothed and General Saw-Teeth and they went by all their secret ways into the storehouse and began to gnaw away at the stone chest, while the cat kept a tight grip on the King of the Rats all through that long night. It was a terrible work. They sharpened their teeth and sharpened them again, and attacked the stone chest. Some of the devoted rats fell dead under the strain, but the rest laboured on to save their King's life, and at last, just before sunrise, the hole was large enough for them to drag the measure out, and through enlarged runways they dragged it into the garden. The cat stretched his stiffened limbs and thanked them gratefully, and the King of the Rats ran back to his loyal subjects.

The cat and the dog carried the measure triumphantly between them until they got to the river, then the cat took it carefully in his mouth while the dog waded into the water. The cat scrambled on to his back and he set off to swim across the wide, swift river. Half-way across he tried to look over his shoulder to see if the cat was holding the measure securely, but he could not turn his head without going under; so he said, 'Have you got it safe still?' The cat said nothing because he was holding on with both his paws, and he dared not open his mouth for fear of dropping the heavy iron measure. So the dog became more and more anxious. 'Have you got the measure safe?' he asked again. Still the cat said nothing. At this the dog became really angry. He stopped swimming, trod water and barked furiously. 'Why don't you answer me?' he said. 'Of course, I've got it!' said the cat. 'Go on, can't you?' For he felt himself sinking. The measure slipped out of his mouth and sank to the bottom of the deep river. There was no chance of getting it up. They swam miserably to shore. When he reached the bank the dog was so ashamed of his folly that he put his tail between his legs and ran home.

The cat dragged himself out of the river and started for home too, and then he thought to himself, 'We are all hungry and my poor old master and mistress will be starving; I will see if I can find anything to bring home for our dinners.' So he turned back to the riverside to see if he could find a fish or any living creature that would serve for a meal. At length he saw a fisherman emptying his nets, and there was one big, heavy, dead fish among the others. The fisherman picked it out and threw it away. The cat thought, 'It is very big. It may make a meal for all of us;' so he dragged it back to the house. It was very hard and heavy, but he put it down with a mew at his mistress's feet. 'Look, good pussy's brought us something for supper!', she said. She picked it up and got a knife. 'How hard and heavy it is!' she said. 'There must be something inside.' And she cut it open. She was right, the measure was inside it. The fish had swallowed it, thinking, no doubt, that he would take it down to the Dragon King, and it had choked him. You can imagine what joy there was at getting the magic measure back again, and having a meal of delicious rice. They could not make enough of the cat. His master said that as a reward he should sleep with him on his bed every night, but because of the dog's folly he would only be allowed to sleep in the yard. The dog was disgusted at such treatment, and from that day to this cats and dogs have glared and growled at each other whenever they have met.[2]

The Chinese have a somewhat similar story, 'The Helpful Animals', with a sad and ironic ending. The magic object here is a fragment of iron hooked up by a young fisherman from the sea, and recognized by him as a sacred treasure. He took it home, hid it in a pot and hung it from a beam. While he possessed it he was magically prosperous so much so that he was rich enough to hire a man-servant to work for him and his wife. All the neighbours knew that this poor couple had become mysteriously rich, and the servant became curious about this. He started to spy on his master and noticed that he venerated an iron pot hanging from the beam. One dark night the evil servant climbed up to the beam and stole away the fragment of iron hidden in it. With this he escaped over the sea back to his old home. The magic property went with him and the man and his wife became as poor as ever.

Now the dog and the cat in the house were much attached to

their master, and one day the cat said to the dog: 'Not so long ago our master used to give us good rice and meat and fish. Why is it that he is so poor again that he can only give us a little soaked rice?' 'It's because master's treasure has been stolen by a thief,' said the dog. 'He has carried it to his house, across a sea and across

a river. I think we should fetch it back.' 'Yes, I think so too,' said the cat. 'Let us go tonight.' So they set off. When they got to the sea the dog did not know what to do. 'Ah,' said the cat, 'cats always have plans.' 'Dogs have plans too,' said the dog, and they both set out together to swim the sea; and they crossed the river in the same way, and followed the thief's scent to his house. 'Now you wait here,' said the cat, 'and I'll creep into the house and get you a bone and drink a little fish soup myself, and then we'll think of a plan to get back the magic fragment.'

So they ate and drank and rested, and about midnight, when the thief and his wife had gone to bed, the cat crept into the house, went to a mousehole, and said to the mice, 'Will you help us to get back the treasure that has been stolen?' 'Certainly,' said the mice. 'But where is it?' 'It is inside that iron box hanging from the beam up there,' said the cat. 'We must consult our adviser,' said the mice. 'He will know what to do.'

The adviser was an old, one-eyed mouse. He told the young mice to climb up to the rafter and gnaw through the rope by which the box was hanging. They swarmed up the walls and began to gnaw. The thief's wife was only half asleep. She pushed her husband. 'What's that gnawing sound?' she said. 'Nothing,' said the thief, only half awake. 'Do get to sleep.' The gnawing went gently on, and presently there was a loud bang as the box fell to the ground. 'There!' said the wife. 'I told you there was something.' 'A clap of thunder,' said the thief, still three-quarters asleep, 'Do let a man get a night's rest.' And they both fell sound asleep. The mice gnawed away at the box, and soon one could slip

41

in and pull out the fragment. They gave it to the cat and dog, who were both very grateful.

On the return journey, they both wanted to take it, but the cat took it because he thought the dog might let it slip. They began to swim across the river, but in the deep water at the far side of the river it slipped out of his mouth. 'There!' said the dog, 'You said I couldn't be trusted, but it was you that dropped it!' The cat said nothing, but dived into the water and caught a water-rat. 'Oh, please don't eat me!' said the water-rat. 'No, I won't eat you,' said the cat, 'if you bring me up that little piece of iron that is lying at the bottom of the stream.' The water-rat dived down and soon brought up the treasure. The cat took the treasure, and they trotted gladly on towards the sea. When they reached the shore the dog said, 'It's my turn to carry it now. You've had it all the way.' The cat did not want to part with it, but he did not want to quarrel with the dog either, so he gave it up. But before they reached the shore the dog somehow let it slip out of his mouth, and down it fell to the bottom of the sea. They scrambled out on to a mud-bank and there they let themselves go. From words it got to blows and soon they were rolling round and round on the mud-bank until they were as filthy as water buffaloes. The din of barking, growling, yowling and spitting disturbed the Dragon King in his palace at the depths of the sea, and he sent a messenger to enquire into the cause of the battle. When he heard it was about a piece of broken iron, he said there was no difficulty about that, for it had just fallen down into his courtyard. He sent it up by the messenger and the two dilapidated animals staggered home and into the house. The cat had the treasure. His mistress was alone. The cat, thickly caked in mud, put his front paws on the table and dropped the piece of iron from his mouth. His mistress hardly noticed it. She saw the two mud-enveloped animals and was filled with fury. She seized a heavy stick. 'You monsters!' she screamed. 'Now we are poor you despise us! You are become as filthy as corpses!' With her first blow she struck the cat dead and with her second the dog. When they were both lifeless the magic treasure slipped back to the sea from which it had come, and all hope of prosperity went with it.[3]

There is no origin legend in this tragic tale, for the cat and dog were both dead, and incapable of carrying on the feud. It only indicates the tendency of the two to disagree in a joint enterprise and the injustice and callousness with which these domestic animals are rewarded by the human beings who are responsible for them. It will be observed that though the cat caught and frightened the water-rat it seemed to be on amicable terms with the mice, perhaps a unique example of such a relationship in folk tradition.

As a rule if a partnership was ever attempted the advantage was all on the cat's side, as we find in the Grimm story of 'The Cat and the Mouse in Partnership'.

A certain cat had made the acquaintance of a mouse, and had said so much to her about the great love and friendship she felt for her, that at length the mouse agreed that they should live and keep house together. 'But we must make a provision for winter, or else we shall suffer from hunger,' said the cat; 'and you, little mouse, cannot venture everywhere, or you will be caught in a trap some day.' The good advice was followed, and a pot of fat was bought, but they did not know where to put it. At length, after much consideration, the cat said: 'I know no place where it will be better stored up than in the church, for no one dares take anything away from there. We will set it beneath the altar, and not touch it until we are really in need of it.' So the pot was placed in safety, but it was not long before the cat had a great yearning for it, and said to the mouse: 'I want to tell you something, little mouse; my cousin has brought a little son into the world, and has asked me to be godmother; he is white with brown spots, and I am to hold him over the font at the christening. Let me go out today, and you look after the house by yourself.' 'Yes, yes,' answered the mouse, 'by all means go, and if you get anything very good to eat, think of me. I should like a drop of sweet red christening wine myself.' All this, however, was untrue; the cat had no cousin, and had not been asked to be godmother. She went straight to the church, stole to the pot of fat, began to lick at it, and licked the top of the fat off. Then she took a walk upon the roofs of the town, looked out for opportunities, and then stretched herself in the sun, and licked her lips whenever she thought of the pot of fat, and not until it was evening did she return home. 'Well, here you are again,' said the mouse, 'no doubt you have had a merry day.' 'All went off well,' answered the cat. 'What name did they give the child?' 'Top off!' said the cat quite coolly. 'Top off!' cried the mouse, 'that is a very odd and uncommon name, is it a usual one in your family?' 'What does that matter,' said the cat, 'it is no worse than Crumb-stealer, as your god-children are called.'

Before long the cat was seized by another fit of yearning. She said to the mouse: 'You must do me a favour, and once more manage the house for a day alone. I am again asked to be godmother, and, as the child has a white ring round its neck, I cannot refuse.' The good mouse consented, but the cat crept behind the town walls to the church, and devoured half the pot of fat. 'Nothing ever seems so good as what one keeps to oneself,' said she, and was quite satisfied with her day's work. When she went home the mouse inquired 'And what was this child christened?' 'Half-done,' answered the cat. 'Half-done! What are you saying? I have never heard the name in my life, I'll wager anything it is not in the calendar!'

The cat's mouth soon began to water for some more licking. 'All good things go in threes,' said she, 'I am asked to stand godmother again. The child is quite black, only it has white paws, but with that exception, it has not a single white hair on its whole body; this only happens once every few years, you will let me go, won't you?' 'Top-off! Half-done!'' answered the mouse, 'They are such odd names, they make me very thoughtful.' 'You sit at home,' said the cat, 'in your dark grey fur coat and long tail, and are filled with fancies, that's because you do not go out in the daytime.' During the cat's absence the mouse cleaned the house, and put it in order, but the greedy cat entirely emptied the pot of fat. 'When everything is eaten up one has some peace,' said she to herself, and well filled and fat she did not return home till night. The mouse at once asked what name had been given to the third child. 'It will not please you more than the other,' said the cat. 'He is called All-gone.' 'All-gone,' cried the mouse, 'that is the most suspicious name of all! I have never seen it in print. All-gone; what can that mean?' and she shook her head, curled herself up, and lay down to sleep.

From this time forth no one invited the cat to be god-mother, but when the winter had come and there was no longer anything to be found outside, the mouse thought of their provision, and said: 'Come, cat, we will go to our pot of fat which we have stored up for ourselves – we shall enjoy that.' 'Yes,' answered the cat, 'you will enjoy it as much as you would enjoy sticking that dainty tongue of yours out of the window.' They set out on their way, but when they arrived, the pot of fat certainly was still in its place, but it was empty. 'Alas!' said the mouse, 'now I see what has happened, now it comes to light! You a true friend! You have devoured all when you were standing godmother. First top off, then half done then –' 'Will you hold your tongue,' cried the cat, 'one word more, and I will eat you too.' 'All gone' was already on the poor mouse's lips; scarcely had she spoken it before the cat sprang on her, seized her, and swallowed her down. Verily, that is the way of the world.[4]

This story shows the cat in the worst light, sly, hypocritical, greedy and ferocious. It is several degrees worse than an ogre to the mice, and since there are almost no giant killers in cat and mouse stories, the mouse rarely wins.

In one tale from Northern Ireland the mouse succeeds in making his escape. It is in Michael J. Murphy's collection, *Now You're Talking*, 'The Cat and the Mouse in a Public House'. It happened one night that a cat was chasing a mouse in the public house and the mouse fell into an open keg of whiskey, and the mouse was drowning in the whiskey, and it kept calling out, 'Save me! Save me'. And the cat said, 'If I pull you out it would just be to eat you.'

'I don't care!' said the mouse, 'Only get me out! I can't endure to die in the drink.'

So the cat reached down into the barrel and it managed to paw the mouse out, and set it down to play with it, and the mouse twisted and turned and at last it came to a hole and popped into it. 'Here!' said the cat, 'Fair play! You promised that if I pulled you out of the whiskey you'd let me eat you.'

The mouse peeped out of the hole and he squeaked, 'Who gives any heed to what a fella says in drink!'[5]

The English version of that story has not the incident of the escape. It is an anecdote of pot valour!

A man had been drinking after dinner, and he was sitting at the table with a few drops of whisky just at the bottom of his glass. Presently a mouse climbed up the tablecloth and ran about the table picking up crumbs. It climbed up the glass, fell inside, and sucked up all the whisky. Then it began dashing round the glass until it knocked it over, stood up unsteadily on its hind legs, brushed back its whiskers, clenched its front paws, and said: 'Now wher'sh that damned cat!'[6]

In one version of the cat and mouse story, preserved in Halliwell's *Nursery Rhymes*, the cat sticks honourably to its bargain, though of course it had no initial right to the mouse's tail.

The cat and the mouse
Play'd in the malt-house.
The cat bit the mouse's tail off. 'Pray, puss, give me my tail.'
'No,' says the cat, 'I'll not give you your tail, till you go to

the cow, and fetch me some milk.'
First she leapt, and then she ran,
Till she came to the cow, and thus began:
'Pray, Cow, give me milk, that I may give cat milk, that
cat may give me my own tail again.' 'No,' said the cow,
'I will give you no milk, till you go to the farmer, and
get me some hay.'
First she leapt, and then she ran,
Till she came to the farmer and thus began:
'Pray, Farmer, give me hay, that I may give cow hay,
That cow may give me milk, that I may give cat milk,
that cat may give me my own tail again.' 'No,'
said the farmer, 'I'll give you no hay, till you go
to the butcher and fetch me some meat.'
First she leapt, and then she ran,
Till she came to the butcher and thus began:
'Pray, Butcher, give me some meat, that I may give
farmer meat, that farmer may give me hay, that I
may give cow hay, that cow may give me milk, that
I may give cat milk, that cat may give me my own
tail again.' 'No,' says the butcher, 'I'll
give you no meat till you go to the baker and
fetch me some bread.
First she leapt and then she ran,
Till she came to the baker and thus began:
'Pray, Baker, give me some bread, that I may give
butcher bread, that butcher may give me meat, that
I may give farmer meat, that farmer may give me
hay, that I may give cow hay, that cow may give me
milk, that I may give cat milk, that cat may give
me my own tail again.'
'Yes,' says the baker, 'I'll give you some bread.
But if you eat my meal I'll cut off your head.'
Then the baker gave mouse bread, and mouse gave
butcher bread, and butcher gave mouse meat, and
mouse gave farmer meat, and farmer gave mouse hay,
and mouse gave cow hay, and cow gave mouse milk,
and mouse gave cat milk, and cat gave mouse her own
tail again![7]

47

This follows the same pattern as the more dramatic and better known 'Old Woman and the Pig'. In both of them the final chain holds good, but in 'The Cat and the Mouse' rewards are promised and each party honours his contract, but in the 'Old Woman and the Pig' the chain is founded on threats and violence. As a child I used to be perturbed by the difficulty of stopping each agent in time, and the dilemma of the butcher, half hanged, the ox half killed, the stick half burnt, and so on. 'The Cat and the Mouse' is a gentler tale.

There are many variants on the 'Mouse and Mouser' situation, one in Jacobs *English Fairy tales*,[8] but perhaps the most poetic is the Scottish version given in Chambers *Popular Rhymes of Scotland*, 'The Cattie sits in the Kiln-Ring Spinning'.[9]

These are true nursery stories, and belong properly to Chapter Eleven.

4
CATS
and Other Creatures as Friends or Foes

In tales and legends cats keep various company, sometimes as companions and sometimes as adversaries. The many variants of the tale best known as 'Bremen Town Musicians',[1] from *Grimm's Fairy Tales*, is one of the commonest in which cats appear in friendly association with other animals. In the Grimm version the animals come together to try to make their own living without the help of any man. They have good reason for this, for all are fugitives from man's ingratitude after years of faithful service. Man's ingratitude to beasts is a common motif in folktales, but some tales of this particular type (130) do not make so much of a feature of this motif, though the Highland version, J. F. Campbell's 'White Pet',[2] has no human companion for the animals, for the same reason as 'The Bremen Musicians'. There are many versions of this tale, with or without a human companion, but Kennedy's tale, 'Jack and his Comrades', though much longer, deserves to be included because of the liveliness and pathos of the descriptions.

Once there was a poor widow, as often there was, and she had one son. A very scarce summer came, and they didn't know how they'd live till the new potatoes would be fit for eating. So Jack said to his mother one evening, 'Mother, bake my cake, and kill my cock, till I go seek my fortune; and if I

meet it, never fear but I'll soon be back to share it with you.'
So she did as he asked her, and he set out at break of day on
his journey. His mother came along with him to the bawn
(yard) gate, and says she – 'Jack, which would you rather
have, half the cake and half the cock with my blessing, or the
whole of 'em with my curse.' 'O musha, mother,' says Jack,
'why do you ax me that question? Sure you know I wouldn't
have your curse and Damer's estate along with it.' 'Well,
then, Jack,' says she, 'here's the whole tote (lot) of 'em, and
my thousand blessings along with them.' So she stood on the
bawn ditch (fence) and blessed him as far as her eyes could
see him.

Well, he went along and along till he was tired, and ne'er a
farmer's house he went into wanted a boy. At last his road
led by the side of a bog, and there was a poor ass up to his
shoulders near a big bunch of grass he was striving to come
at. 'Ah, then, Jack asthore,' says he, 'help me out or I'll be
dhrownded.' 'Never say't twice,' says Jack, and he pitched in
big stones and scraws (sods) into the slob, till the ass got
good ground under him. 'Thank you, Jack,' says he, when he
was out on the hard road; 'I'll do as much for you another
time, Where are you going?' 'Faith, I'm going to seek my
fortune till harvest comes in, God bless it!' 'And if you like,'
says the ass, 'I'll come along with you; who knows what luck
we may have!' 'With all my heart; it's getting late, let us be
jogging.'

Well, they were going through a village, and a whole army
of gossoons were hunting a poor dog with a kittle tied to his
tail. He ran up to Jack for protection, and the ass let such a
roar out of him, that the little thieves took to their heels as if
the ould boy (the devil) was after them. 'More power to you,
Jack!' says the dog. 'I'm much obleeged to you: where is the
baste and yourself going?' 'We're going to seek our fortune
till harvest comes in.' 'And wouldn't I be proud to go with
you!' says the dog, 'and get shut (rid) of them ill-conducted
boys; purshuin' to 'em!' 'Well, well, throw your tail over
your arm and come along.'

They got outside the town, and sat down under an old
wall, and Jack pulled out his bread and meat, and shared with

the dog; and the ass made his dinner on a bunch of thistles. While they were eating and chatting, what should come by but a poor half-starved cat, and the moll-row he gave out of him would make your heart ache. 'You look as if you saw the tops of nine houses since breakfast,' says Jack; 'here's a bone and something on it.' 'May your child never know a hungry belly!' says Tom; 'It's myself that's in need of your kindness. May I be so bold as to ask where yez are all going?' 'We're going to seek our fortune till the harvest comes in, and you may join us if you like.' 'And that I'll do with a heart and a half,' says the cat, 'and thank'ee for asking me.'

Off they set again, and just as the shadows of the trees were three times as long as themselves, they heard a great cackling in a field beside the road, and out over the ditch jumped a fox with a fine black cock in his mouth. 'Oh, you anointed villain!' says Jack, and the word wasn't out of his mouth when Coley was in full sweep after the Moddhera Rua (Red Dog). Reynard dropped his prize like a hot potato, and was off like shot, and the poor cock came back fluttering and trembling to Jack and his comrades. 'O musha, naybours!' says he, 'wasn't it the hoith o' luck that threw you in my way! Maybe I won't remember your kindness if ever I find you in hardship; and where in the world are you all going?' 'We're going to seek our fortune till the harvest comes in; you may join our party if you like, and sit on Neddy's crupper when your legs and wings are tired.'

Well, the march began again, and just as the sun was gone down they looked round, and there was neither cabin nor farmhouse in sight. 'Well, well,' says Jack, 'the worse luck now the better another time, and it's only a summer night after all. We'll go into the wood and make our bed on the long grass.' No sooner said than done. Jack stretched himself on a bunch of dry grass, the ass lay near him, the dog and cat lay in the ass's warm lap, and the cock went to roost in the next tree.

Well, the soundness of deep sleep was over them all, when the cock took a notion of crowing. 'Bother you, Cuileach Dhu (Black Cock)!' says the ass: 'you disturbed me from as nice a wisp of hay as ever I tasted. What's the matter?' 'It's daybreak, that's the matter: don't you see light yonder?' 'I see a light indeed,' says Jack, 'but it's from a candle it's coming, and not from the sun. As you've roused us we may as well go over, and ask for lodging.' So they all shook themselves, and went on through grass, and rocks, and briars, till they got down into a hollow, and there was the light coming through the shadow, and along with it came singing, and laughing, and cursing. 'Easy, boys!' says Jack: 'walk on your tippy toes till we see what sort of people we have to deal with.' So they crept near the window, and there they saw six robbers inside, with pistols, and blunderbushes, and cutlashes, sitting at a table, eating roast beef and pork, and drinking mulled beer, and wine, and whisky punch.

'Wasn't that a fine haul we made at the lord of Dunlavin's!' says one ugly-looking thief with his mouth full, 'and it's little we'd get only for the honest porter: here's his purty health!' 'The porter's purty health!' cried out every one of them, and Jack bent his finger at his comrades. 'Close your ranks, my men,' says he in a whisper, 'and let every one mind the word of command.' So the ass put his fore-hoofs on the sill of the window, the dog got on the ass's head, the cat got on the dog's head, and the cock on the cat's head. Then Jack made a sign, and they all sung out like mad. 'Hee-haw, hee-haw!' roared the ass; 'bow-wow!' barked the dog; 'meaw-meaw!' cried the cat; 'cock-a-doodle-doo!' crowed the cock. 'Level your pistols!' cried Jack, 'and make smithereens of 'em. Don't leave a mother's son of 'em alive; present, fire!' With that they gave another halloo, and smashed every pane in the window. The robbers were frightened out of their lives. They blew out the candles, threw down the table, and skelped out at the back door as if they were in earnest, and never drew rein till they were in the very heart of the wood.

Jack and his party got into the room, closed the shutters, lighted the candles, and ate and drank till hunger and thirst were gone. Then they lay down to rest; – Jack in the bed, the ass in the stable, the dog on the door mat, the cat by the fire, and the cock on the perch.

At first the robbers were very glad to find themselves in the thick wood, but they soon began to get vexed. 'This damp grass is very different from our warm room,' says one; 'I was obliged to drop a fine pig's crubeen (foot),' says another; 'I didn't get a tay-spoonful of my last tumbler,' says another; 'and all the Lord of Dunlavin's gold and silver that we left behind!' says the last. 'I think I'll venture back,' says the captain, 'and see if we can recover anything.' 'What a good boy!' said they all, and away he went.

The lights were all out, and so he groped his way to the fire, and there the cat flew in his face, and tore him with teeth and claws. He let a roar out of him, and made for the room door, to look for a candle inside. He trod on the dog's tail, and if he did, he got the marks of his teeth in his arms, and legs, and thighs. 'Millia murdher (thousand murders)!' cried he; 'I wish I was out of this unlucky house.' When he got to the street door, the cock dropped down upon him with his claws and bill, and what the cat and dog done to him was only a flay–bite to what he got from the cock. 'Oh, tattheration to you all, you unfeeling vagabonds!' says he, when he recovered his breath; and he staggered and spun round and round till he reeled into the stable, back foremost, but the ass received him with a kick on the broadest part of his small clothes, and laid him comfortably on the dunghill. When he came to himself, he scratched his head, and began to think what happened to him; and as soon as he found that his legs were able to carry him, he crawled away, dragging one foot after another, till he reached the wood.

'Well, well,' cried them all, when he came within hearing, 'any chance of our property?' 'You may say chance,' says he, 'and it's itself is the poor chance all out. Ah, will any of you pull a bed of dry grass for me? All the sticking plaster in Inniscorfy (Enniscorthy) will be too little for the cuts and bruises I have on me. Ah, if you only knew what I've gone through for you! When I got to the kitchen fire, looking for a sod of lighted turf, what should be there but a colliach (old woman) carding flax, and you may see the marks she left on my face with the cards. I made to the room door as fast as I could, and who should I stumble over but a cobbler and his seat, and if he did not work at me with his awls and his pinchers you may call me a rogue. Well, I got away from him somehow, but when I was passing through the door, it must be the divel himself that pounced down on me with his claws, and his teeth, that were equal to sixpenny nails, and his wings – ill luck be in his road! Well, at last I reached the stable, and there, by the way of salute, I got a pelt from a sledge-hammer that sent me half a mile off. If you don't believe me, I'll give you leave to go and judge for yourselves.' 'Oh, my poor captain,' says they, 'we believe you to the nines. Catch us, indeed, going within a hen's race of that unlucky cabin!'

Well, before the sun shook his doublet next morning, Jack and his comrades were up and about. They made a hearty breakfast on what was left the night before, and then they all agreed to set off to the castle of the Lord of Dunlavin, and give him back all his gold and silver. Jack put it all in the two ends of a sack, and laid it across Neddy's back, and all took the load in their hands. Away they went, through bogs, up hills, down dales, and sometimes along the yalla high road, till they came to the hall door of the Lord of Dunlavin, and who should be there, airing his powdered head, his white stockings, and his red breeches, but the thief of a porter.

He gave a cross look to the visitors, and says he to Jack, 'What do you want here, my fine fellow? There isn't room for you all.' 'We want,' says Jack, 'what I'm sure you haven't to give us – and that is, common civility.' 'Come, be off, you lazy geochachs (greedy strollers)!' says he, 'while a cat 'ud be licking her ear, or I'll let the dogs at you.' 'Would you tell a body,' says the cock that was perched on the ass's head, 'who was it that opened the door for the robbers the other night?' Ah! maybe the porter's red face didn't turn the colour of his frill, and the Lord of Dunlavin and his pretty daughter, that were standing at the parlour window unknownst to the porter, put out their heads. 'I'd be glad, Barney,' says the master, 'to hear your answer to the gentleman with the red comb on him.' 'Ah, my lord, don't belief the rascal; sure I didn't open the door to the six robbers.' 'And how did you know there were six, you poor innocent?' says the lord. 'Never mind, sire,' says Jack, 'all your gold and silver is there in that sack, and I don't think you will begrudge us our supper and bed after our long march from the road of Athsalach (muddy ford).' 'Begrudge, indeed! Not one of you will ever see a poor day if I can help it.'

So all were welcomed to their heart's content, and the ass, and the dog, and the cock got the best posts in the farmyard, and the cat took possession of the kitchen. The lord took Jack in hand, dressed him from top to toe in broadcloth, and frills as white as snow, and turnpumps, and put a watch in his fob. When they sat down to dinner, the lady of the house said Jack had the air of a born gentleman about him, and the lord said he'd make him his steward. Jack brought his mother, and settled her comfortably near the castle, and all were as happy as you please. The old woman that told me the story said Jack and the young lady were married; but if they were, I hope he spent two or three years getting the edication of a gentleman. I don't think that a country boy would feel comfortable, striving to find discourse for a well-bred young lady, the length of a summer's day, even if he had the Academy of Compliments, and the Complete Letter Writer by heart.[3]

Kennedy notes that this last reference to the chapbook literature of his period was made by the narrator of the tale, whose style and diction he reproduced.

A quiet, peaceful version of this tale, listed as type 130, is given in Genevieve Massignon's volume in the Folktales of the World

Series. 'The Four Friends' of the tale are a goose, a cat, a heifer and a lamb. There are no robbers in it nor combat of any kind, as in The Bremen Musicians. The four friends, setting out for the mountains of Cervières, do not travel further than their first night's stopping place, where they are gladly taken in and adopted by a lonely old woman. It is a bedtime story fit to soothe the nerves of the most timid and excitable child. It comes from the Province of Forey.[4]

There is a strange association of creatures put together in a Welsh fable recorded by Elias Owen in *Welsh Folk-Lore*. It is almost impossible to believe that this was ever a serious origin legend; it seems to be a play of folk fancy. Elias Owen describes the occasion on which he heard the fable.

'It is from thirty to forty years ago that I heard the fable I am about to relate, and the circumstances under which I heard it are briefly as follows. I was walking towards Bangor from Llanllachid, when I saw a farmer at work hedging. I stopped to chat with him, and a bramble which had fastened itself on his trousers gave him a little trouble to get it away, and the man in a pet said, "Have I not paid my tithe?" "Why do you say those words, Enoch?" said I, and he said, "Have you not heard the story?" I confessed my ignorance, and after many preliminary remarks, the farmer related the following fable:

'The heron, the cat, and the bramble bought the tithe of a certain parish. The heron bought the hay, mowed it, harvested it, and cocked it, and intended carrying it the following day, but in the night a storm came on, and carried the hay away, and ever since then the heron frequents the banks of the rivers and lakes looking for her hay that was carried away, and saying, "Pay me my tithe."

'The cat bought the oats, cut them and even threshed them, and left them in the barn, intending the following day to take them to the market for sale. But when she went into the barn early the next morning, she found the floor covered with rats and mice, which had devoured the oats, and the cat flew at them and fought with them, and drove them from the barn, and this is why she is at enmity with rats and mice even to this day.

'The bramble bought the wheat, and was more fortunate than the heron and the cat, for the wheat was bagged, and taken to the market and sold, but sold on trust, and the bramble never got the money, and this is why it takes hold of everyone and says, "Pay me my tithe" for it forgot to whom the wheat had been sold.'[5]

Apparently in Wales in those days the tithes on different crops could be sold separately to speculators, a complicated and inconvenient custom.

A Greek version of 'The Helpful Animals' and 'The Cat and the Dog' quoted in Chapter Three introduces a snake as the third character. A little 'Cinder-lad', Cinderillo, on three different occasions spends a farthing given by his mother to save the lives of three animals, a dog, a cat and a snake. He takes them to his home and looks after them. The first to show his gratitude is the snake, the son of the King of the Snakes, who invites Cinderillo to his home and advises him to ask for a certain talisman, a little ring which the King Snake keeps under his tongue, who gives it to him in gratitude for saving his son. It turns out to be a wishing ring and with it Cinderillo wins the hand of the Princess, performing various feats laid down by the King, among them the building of a beautiful tower close to the Palace. Here Cinderillo and the Princess lived after their marriage, guarded by a blackamoor.

The Princess, however, did not like Cinderillo and fell in love with the blackamoor. Cinderillo kept the ring under his tongue for safety, as the King Snake had done, but the Princess knew about it, and stole it for the blackamoor guard. The servant of the ring transferred his allegiance to his new master, as these ring slaves are bound to do. In the morning Cinderillo waked to find himself lying by the roadside, and the magic tower had been transported to the middle of the sea with the Princess and the blackamoor inside it. Cinderillo bewailed himself to the King and then went back to his old home, but he soon set out to look for his bride, taking his young dog and cat with him.

The next part of the story follows the same pattern as 'The Cat and the Dog' – the dog carries the cat on his back to the tower; the cat induces a mouse to steal the ring, kept by the blackamoor in his mouth. The mouse does it very artfully by dipping his tail in honey and rubbing it in pepper; then putting it up the sleeping blackamoor's nose. As in the other stories the ring was lost in the ocean and recovered by the cat from a fish. Cinderillo used the

ring to have the tower with its occupants carried back, the infuriated King killed both the blackamoor and the Princess, and subsequently married Cinderillo to his second daughter. They lived happily in the tower with the cat and the dog until Cinderillo inherited the throne. It is noticeable that the cat and the dog are the two helpful animals, and the snake shows his gratitude by the gift of the ring and plays no part in rescuing it.[6]

Curiously enough, there are many tales of cats collaborating with other animals but there are a few of their coming into conflict with them. Occasionally a cat comes into collision with a fox, as he did in 'The Four Friends'. In an Eastern European tale, for instance, the cat, the cock and the fox live together. While the cat is out in the forest, the fox carries off the cock, who cackles so loudly that the cat hears him, and dashes back to the rescue. He punishes the fox by luring the cubs out of their hole with his music and killing them.[7] In a milder encounter the fox taunts the cat with knowing only one trick whilst he knows a hundred. The cat retorts that his one trick is worth a hundred of the fox's. While they are disputing the baying of the hounds is heard in the distance and the cat runs up a tree out of reach of the pack, while the fox tries all his hundred tricks in turn, and is caught at last. The story is widely known in Germany, Scandinavia and through most of Europe. A modern Irish version of it is to be found in Michael Murphy's collection of folktales, *Now You're Talking*.[8]

The Japanese tale of 'The Cat and the Crab' is a form of the common type of a race between two animals, of which one is fast and the other slow. Aesop's 'Hare and the Tortoise' is perhaps the best-known example, but here it is a straight-forward competition between determined perseverance and overweening conceit. In most of the stories, however, some element of cheating is introduced. As a rule, for instance, as in 'The Hare and the Stickly-Backed Urchin', the race is run along parallel furrows and the slower animal posts a relative at the other end. In the Japanese version the cat imagines himself well able to outrun the sidling crab. Indeed he goes ahead at the first leap, but the astute crab catches hold of his tail and is carried all down the course. When he gets to the winning post the cat wheels round to see how far he has got; the crab looses his hold and is standing neatly just beyond the winning post. There appear to be no umpires, and the cat suspects no trickery and concedes the victory. Here the cat is a less wily character than in most folktales.[9]

In 'The End of Brer Anansi' from Lucille Iremonger's collection
of *West Indian Folk-Tales*, the cat is in more than his ordinary
form, though it is only fair to say that Brer Anansi deserved
everything that he got. Brer Anansi, the spider's god, is a trickster
figure, usually in the form of a little fat, bald, black man, though
he can take the shape of a spider at will. He is a thief and a
trickster, but he is a particularly malicious character, and the
world was well rid of him when he met his match in Brer Puss.

One day Brer Puss set out on a long journey. He walked and
walked until he came to a river. There he halted, for there
was no bridge for him to walk over. He was afraid of the
water, and he could not swim. In the end he climbed a tree
to sit and think out a plan.

As Brer Puss walked along the branches, looking for a nice
place on which to lie, he caught sight of Brer Anansi below
him on the bank of the river. Brer Anansi was fishing. He
was doing well, too. Every now and then he would pull in
his line, take a fish from the hook, and put it into his bag.

Brer Puss was very interested, and he lay along a branch
and kept watch up in the tree.

Brer Puss was very fond of fish!

Brer Anansi came up the river, fishing, until he stood right
under Brer Puss's tree. But Brer Puss did not call out to him.

At last Brer Anansi laid down his rod, shut up his bag, and
went to stretch his legs along the bank of the river. Brer
Anansi felt hungry, but he was too lazy to get himself any
food or to cook his fish. However, as he was walking along
he came across a stump of a tree in which some bees had
made a hive. The honey was oozing down its sides. Brer
Anansi stopped to have a look at it. He licked his lips and
thought how lucky he was to have discovered it just when he
was ready for his dinner. He began to lick all the honey from
the outside of the stump.

And all the time Brer Puss kept watch up in his tree.

If there is all this honey running down outside the stump then there must be a great deal more inside it! Brer Anansi said to himself, and he put his hand inside the hole from which the honey was oozing. Immediately something inside the stump caught hold of his hand. Brer Anansi was very, very frightened. He could not see anyone or anything, and he could not tell who it was that was holding him. He tried to pull his hand away, and he turned and he twisted, but he could not get away.

At last he called out, 'Who holds me?'

Then a terrible voice came out of the stump.

'I am the Hurler. I hold you!'

'Let me go!' cried Brer Anansi. 'Let me go!'

But the voice only said again, 'I am the Hurler. I hold you!'

Then Brer Anansi cried, 'O Hurler, hurl me with all your might!'

The Hurler spun Brer Anansi in the air and flung him far away.

Luckily for Brer Anansi, he fell into a little bush, and so he was not killed. He sat exactly where he had fallen for a long time, and he thought and he thought and he thought.

And all the time Brer Puss kept watch up in his tree.

At last Brer Anansi got up from where he was sitting. He pulled up the little bush, and in its place he put a heap of stones and pointed stakes. Then he sat down and waited to see what would happen.

And all the time Brer Puss kept watch up in his tree.

A little later Sister Hen came by.

'Good morning, good morning, Sister Hen!' called Brer Anansi.

'Good morning, Brer Anansi. What are you doing here?'

'I have discovered a wonderful secret, Sister Hen!'

'Is that so, Brer Anansi? What is it?'

'Come, and I will show you.'

Brer Anansi led Sister Hen to the stump of the tree.

'Look! Do you see that hole there?' he asked her.

'Yes, Brer Anansi. I see that hole.'

'Well, just put your hand in it, and see what happens!'

Sister Hen pushed her hand inside the hole. The Hurler held her fast.

'Oh! Oh!' Sister Hen cackled. 'Let me go! Let me go!'

'Pull!' said Brer Anansi. 'Pull hard, Sister Hen!'

Sister Hen pulled as hard as she could, but she could not free herself.

'Something is holding me!' she said.

Brer Anansi laughed and laughed to himself, and then he said:

'Say "Who holds me?"'

'Who holds me?' asked Sister Hen.

'I am the Hurler. I hold you!' said the voice.

'Now say, "O Hurler, hurl me with all your might!"' said Brer Anansi.

'O Hurler, hurl me with all your might!' cried Sister Hen.

The Hurler spun Sister Hen round and round, and flung her with all his might. Sister Hen hurtled through the air and fell on the heap of stakes and stones which Brer Anansi had prepared.

Brer Anansi walked over to the heap and picked up Sister Hen and put her in the bag with the fish he had caught.

Then he sat down again and waited to see what would happen next.

And all the time Brer Puss kept watch up in his tree.

Brer Puss was very fond of chicken too!

Brer Rat was the next to come by.

'Good morning, Brer Rat!' Brer Anansi called. 'Good morning, good morning! I was hoping I would meet an honest man!'

'Why?' Brer Rat asked.

'I have found something that will interest you, Brer Rat.'

'You don't say so!' Brer Rat replied. 'What could that be?'

Brer Anansi led Brer Rat straight to the tree-stump.

'Do you see that hole there?' asked Brer Anansi. 'Just push your hand into it and see what you get!'

Brer Rat pushed his hand into the hole. The Hurler held him fast.

'Pull! Pull hard!' cried Brer Anansi. 'As hard as you can!'

'I am pulling as hard as I can,' said Brer Rat, 'but I cannot get away. Is this a trick, Brer Anansi? Something is holding me.'

'Ask "Who holds me?"' Brer Anansi said.

'Who holds me?' Brer Rat asked.

'I am the Hurler. I hold you!' the voice replied.

'Now say, "O Hurler, hurl me with all your might!"' Brer Anansi said.

'O Hurler, hurl me with all your might!' Brer Rat cried.

Then the Hurler whirled Brer Rat round and flung him with all his might and main. Brer Rat fell right on the heap of stakes and stones.

Brer Anansi walked over to the heap, picked up Brer Rat, and put him in the bag with the fish and the chicken. Then he sat down and waited once more to see what would happen next.

And all the time Brer Puss kept watch up in his tree.

Brer Puss was very fond of rat too!

When Brer Anansi's back was turned Brer Puss got down from his tree.

He walked back the way he had come a long way, then he turned round and came back along the path. Brer Anansi saw him coming, and he was glad to see him, for he did not like Brer Puss.

'Walk up, my good friend, Brer Puss!' he called. 'Come and see the fine treasure I have found for me and you!'

'I wonder what that could be, Brer Anansi?' Brer Puss replied quietly.

Brer Anansi led Brer Puss up to his stump and pointed to the hole.

'See that hole there, Brer Puss?' asked Brer Anansi.

'What hole?' asked Brer Puss, looking in the wrong place.

'This hole here,' said Brer Anansi. 'No, here!'

Brer Puss again looked the wrong way.

'No, not there – here, Brer Puss!' said Brer Anansi, getting annoyed. 'Come, put your hand here in this hole!'

Brer Puss deliberately put his hand in the wrong place. Time and again he did this, and again and again Brer Anansi showed him the way. Each time Brer Puss got it wrong, Brer Anansi got more and more angry with him. Brer Puss simply could not find the right place.

At last, when Brer Anansi was trying to show him the hole with a flourish, his own hand went too near it, and the Hurler held it.

Brer Anansi began to cry, for he knew that this time he would not get away alive.

'Brer Puss, go down the path a little way, and you will find some stakes and stones,' he said. 'Pull up the stakes, and scatter the stones, and put down some soft grass. Be quick, and do exactly as I say.'

Brer Puss strolled off to the heap of stones, but he did not scatter them, nor did he pull up the stakes, and he did not lay down any soft grass. He only stood and looked.

Then he went back to where Anansi stood, still held fast by the Hurler.

'Have you put down the grass for me?' Brer Anansi asked anxiously. 'Have you pulled up the stakes, and scattered the stones?'

'Everything is ready for you,' Brer Puss replied.

But Brer Anansi was not satisfied.

'Dear Brer Puss,' he begged, 'go and bring me one of the stakes so that I can be sure!'

Brer Puss strolled away again. He was away a long time,

but he came back without anything.

'Where is it?' Brer Anansi asked.

'The stakes are too heavy for me to bring,' Brer Puss replied. 'I have rolled them out of the way.'

Still Anansi was not satisfied. But he felt the Hurler's strong hand drawing him. He knew that the time had come.

'Who holds me?' he cried.

'I am the Hurler. I hold you!' the voice replied.

Then in a very little, trembling voice Brer Anansi said:

'O Hurler, hurl me with all your might!'

The Hurler lifted Brer Anansi and whirled him round and round in the air and flung him with all his might and main. And Brer Anansi fell scrunch! on to the heap of stakes and stones that he himself had placed there for his enemies.

Brer Puss walked over to the heap of stones. He picked up Brer Anansi and put him into the bag with Brer Rat, Sister Hen, and the fish. Then he put the bag on his back and walked away with it.

And that was the end of Brer Anansi.

Jack Mandory, the story is ended.[10]

5
GOOD LUCK
AND
Bad Luck

The superstitious beliefs about cats are so fragmented and various that it is difficult to make any sense of them. The ancient medical use of cat's blood, powdered flesh, and hair seems to show that they were believed to have life-giving and healing properties, but at the same time it was thought to be dangerous to caress them, inhale their breath, or allow them to walk over one. The same contradictory beliefs are held about the good or bad luck of cats, and in various places different colours are considered ominous or fortunate.

On the whole black cats are believed to be lucky in Britain and white cats unlucky. In parts of America, in Belgium, Spain and in several other countries of Europe white is the lucky colour. The enchanted princess, The White Cat in Mme d'Aulnoy's fairy story, seems to suggest that the same belief is held in France. In England white animals are supposed to be ominous. In the West Country, for instance, it is very unlucky to see a wild white rabbit. It may be that these animals are supposed to be ghosts.

William Henderson, in *Folklore from the Northern Counties*, says that black cats are lucky, but he says at the same time that they are almost inseparable companions of witchcraft. To this he adds several beliefs about the favourability of black cats.

It is curious that at Scarborough, a few years back, sailors' wives liked to keep black cats in their homes, to ensure the

66

safety of their husbands at sea. This gave black cats such a value that no one else could keep them; they were always stolen.[1]

In the face of this it is strange that sailors, and particularly fishermen, have a taboo against mentioning the word cat, either on the way to sea or on board, though it is very lucky to have a cat, and especially a black cat, on the ship. In a wreck the cat is usually one of the first creatures saved.[2] It is unlucky to mention a woman at sea, and even unlucky to meet one on the way to one's boat. Ruth Tongue's story of 'The Four-Eyed Cat', from the Essex sea coasts, combines the woman and the cat in close association with witchcraft, and is also relevant to the belief that cats can raise storms.

There was a gentleman had a beautiful daughter who was bad

at heart, and they said she knew more than a Christian should, and they wanted to swim her, but no one dared because of her father. She drew a spell on a poor fisherman, and he followed for love of her wherever she went. He deserted his troth-plight maid, though he was to be married in a week, and he ran away to sea with the gentleman's daughter, and unbeknown to all the rest (that is, the rest of the fleet) took her out with them to the fishing. She did it to spite her father's pride, but he thought himself well rid of her.

A storm blew up and the whole fishing fleet were lost to a man, for they had on board a woman with them at sea, though none knew of it but her lover. It was she that had whistled up the storm that had drowned her own lover, for she hated everyone. She was turned into a four-eyed cat, and ever after she haunted the herring fleet.

So that is why even now fishermen won't cast their nets before half-past three (cockcrow) – my uncles won't – and they always throw a bit back into the sea for the cat.[3]

This story was told to Ruth Tongue by a girl of thirteen, the daughter of a lightship sailor at Harwich. It is clear that the witch's ghost became a kind of sea demon, which had to be placated by a tribute from the catch.

The Cornish miners have a more stringent cat taboo than the sailors. Not only do they refuse to mention a cat while down the mine, but if a cat should by any chance find its way underground they will not work on that level until it has been killed.[4]

Another hazardous profession, which accordingly suffered from a number of superstitions, is the actor's. Actors think it lucky to have a cat in the theatre, but they say it is unlucky if one crosses the stage during a performance. It certainly distracts the attention of the audience if this happens at a dramatic moment. It is also unlucky for an actor to kick a cat.[5]

Though black cats were associated with witchcraft they were on the whole supposed to be lucky. Mary Trevelyan in *Folk-Lore and Folk-Stories of Wales* has a short passage on cats in which their fortunate and beneficient qualities are given some prominence. She says:

Cats were supposed to be endowed with magical powers, and therefore granted many privileges and indulgences. It was not considered lucky for the inmates of a house to be without a cat.

Girls are told to feed their cats well, so that the sun may shine on their wedding-day. Black cats keep care and trouble away from the house. It is lucky for a black and strange cat to stray into anybody's house, If a black cat is lost, trouble and sorrow will fall upon the house.

A white cat is considered to be unlucky in most parts of the country, but Mary Trevelyan reports that it is very fortunate to have a purely white and a thoroughly black cat in the house.[6] I have myself come across some corroboration of this in the Cotswold area. A neighbour acquired a white cat and was told it would be unlucky to keep it unless the effect was neutralized by also keeping a black one. She therefore procured a black one, very similar to the white in everything except colour.

Henderson mentions several beliefs in the North which corroborate the Welsh superstitions. He quotes two little rhymes from *The Denham Note-Books*.

Kiss the black cat
An' 'twill make ye fat:
Kiss the white ane,
An' 'twill make ye lean.[7]

And about the black cat as propitious to true love he quotes:

> Wherever the cat of the house is black
> The lasses o' lovers will have no lack.

To confirm this he cites oral testimony:
'An old north-country woman said lately to a lady, 'Na wonder Jock's lasses marry off so fast, ye ken what a braw black cat they've got.' He adds, 'Naturally enough it is considered very lucky for a cat of this kind to come of her own accord and take up her residence in any house.'[8]

S. O. Addy, in *Household Tales and Other Traditional Remains*, a collection drawn from York, Lincoln, Derby and Nottingham, reports very similar beliefs, but more briefly. He says:

> It is good for a black cat to come to your house; on no
> account should it be driven away. When you flit or move to
> another house it is unlucky for you to take the cat with you.
> It is all right if the cat follows you of its own accord. It is
> bad for one's health to fondle cats.

He also gives a piece of weather forecasting. 'When the mark (the pupil) of a cat's eye broadens there will be rain.'[9] So many weather forecasts are based on cat behaviour as to remind one of the anxious watch kept by the Egyptian priests over the minutest detail of the temple-cat's behaviour. Some of these seem slightly conflicting. Henderson quotes:

> If the cat washes her face o'er the ear,
> 'Tis a sign that weather'll fair and clear.[10]

In Scotland, on the other hand, if a cat passes its paw over both ears in washing it is thought to be a sign of rain. In Shetland, as we learn in John Spence's *Shetland Folk-Lore*, a cat sitting with her back to the fire was taken as a sign of cold weather on the way, and if she used both forepaws to wash her face it was a certain prognostic of rain. On the other hand, if she slept curled up with her head hidden, fine weather was on the way.[11]

In Hulme's *Natural History Lore and Legend* the cat is supposed to do more than prognosticate bad weather, it creates it. Speaking of cats on shipboard he says:

It was held that they had power to raise a gale, and on board ship the malevolent disposition with which they were credited has made them in an especial degree unpopular shipmates. Pussy was thought to particularly provoke a storm by playing with any article of wearing apparel, by rubbing her face, or by licking her fur the wrong way; she was sheltered from rough usage however by the belief that provoking her would bring a gale, while drowning her would cause a regular tempest.[12]

Mary Trevelyan says that when cats are frisky wind and rain may be expected, and when they sit with their back to the fire snow is coming. They are supposed to divine more than the weather. When they trim their whiskers guests may be expected, when a cat stretches its paws towards the fire strangers are approaching the house. If a cat sneezes once near the bride on her wedding morning it is the omen of a happy married life. Cats sneeze for rain, too, and it used to be believed that if a cat sneezed three times colds and illness would spread through the house.[13] In Radford and Hole's *Encyclopedia of Superstitions* the belief is given in more detail.

An old and cruel superstition said that when a cat fell ill it should be put outside at once because its sickness, even if not infectious, would run right through the house. So too, a dying cat was often thrust outside for fear that Death, when it came for the animal, would stay for some member of the family also.[14]

The cat was credited with a psychic or prophetic consciousness of the approach of death.

If a cat leaves a house when there is illness within, and will not be coaxed back, the sick person will die, and so will he if he dreams of cats, or of two cats fighting. It is often said that cats will temporarily desert a house while there is an unburied corpse in it, returning only after the funeral. If one jumps over the coffin, it is a bad omen for the dead man's soul, unless the poor creature is killed at once.[15]

A dog that does so is killed in the same way.

Here we see the cat seen in an ominous and malefic light, as in the belief that cats may smother small babies by lying on them, or kill them by sucking their breath.[16]

In Wales they say that the house cat knows whether the soul of his dead master has gone to Heaven or Hell. If immediately after a death it climbs up a tree it means that the dead man has gone to Heaven, but if it descends it, the destination is to Hell.[17]

Cats were much used in folk medicine. It was believed that a stye could be cured by stroking it with a black cat's tail. In this spell the cat had to be of the opposite sex to the patient, and the spell was accompanied by a charm (given in Radford and Hole).

> I poke thee, I don't poke thee,
> I poke the queff that's under the ee,
> O qualyway, O qualyway!

The tail is drawn down over the eye at each line of the verse. A tortoiseshell cat's tail does as well, for tortoiseshells are lucky in England.[18] Three drops of cat's blood smeared over a wart were supposed to send it away.[19] In the Highlands of Scotland the cure for erisypilas was blood from a cat's ear.[20] In Pennsylvania in 1867 an old woman was charged with witchcraft for giving a child three drops of blood from a cat's tail as a cure for croup. She acknowledged the fact, but stoutly denied that it was witchcraft.[21] A dried cat's skin held to the face was used as a remedy for toothache, and in the seventeenth century a cat's body, boiled in olive oil, was thought to be an excellent dressing for wounds.[22] A magical method of transferring an illness was to throw a basin of water in which the patient had been washed over the cat and to drive it out of the house.[23]

John Spence, in *Shetland Folk-Lore*, gives a full account of the complicated method by which a cow, presumed to be 'hurt frae the grund' – that is 'elf-shot' – was disenchanted by Maron, a well-reputed witch doctor. It was done by means of a pot of tar, a burning torch, a sacred needle, three little living crabs and a cat.

The poor cow was almost too weak to stand, but Maron got her to her feet with pricks of the needle, and the smoke of the torch, holding the sacred page over her all the time. She set light to the tar and fumigated the poor creature. Then she dragged the cat by its tail three times over the cow's body from head to tail and forced the cow to swallow the three little crabs alive. The shock of

this treatment was supposed to deliver the cow from the dominion of the trows. The cow had the worst of it, but it was rough treatment for the cat too. However, neither life nor sufferings were spared in this rough folk medicine.[24] Hulme, as well as mentioning the cure of a stye by stroking with a black cat's tail and of warts with hairs of a tortoiseshell cat in the month of May, tells us that a whitlow can be cured by holding the affected finger in the cat's ear for a quarter of an hour daily. To improve eyesight it was recommended to burn the head of a black cat into ashes and blow a little of the dust into the eyes every day. This seems a curious remedy, since the brains of a cat were supposed to be a deadly poison, and the smallest quantity of them introduced into a meal was a sure means of getting rid of an enemy.[25] As a formerly sacred animal the cat was used to give fertility to the ground. Cats were buried under fruit trees to ensure a good crop and sacrificed in cornfields for the same reason.

Elias Owen in *Welsh Folk-Lore*, published in 1896, gives divergent opinions about black cats in two verses which he translates into English. The first is favourable:

> A black cat, I've heard it said,
> Can charm all ill away,
> And keep the house wherein she dwells
> From fever's deadly sway.

The second is unfavourable:

> Never keep about thy house
> A white cock or black puss.

He has also a couplet warning against May cats.

> Cats born in May
> Bring snakes to the house.[26]

This seems a pretty general belief, for Ruth Tongue mentions it as being held in Somerset.

> May is an unlucky time for birth. May cats catch no mice, and one is well-advised to drown May kittens at birth, for they will take toads and spiders into the house, and those that do so are not natural cats but witches in disguise.[27]

In Sussex, and many other counties of England, there was another season unlucky for birth. This was just after Michaelmas, when the blackberry season was over. Kittens born at that time were called 'blackberry kits' and were supposed to be particularly wild and mischievous. This is accounted for by Christian Hole in the *Encyclopedia of Superstitions* by the date of the Devil's expulsion from Heaven. It is supposed to have taken place on 10 September, and he bore a particular grudge against blackberries because he landed in a bramble brake on his way to Hell. Ever since then, on the anniversary of his fall, he has travelled the earth fouling the blackberries.[28] At one time they were never picked, and in Brittany and Normandy beautiful blackberries may be seen hanging untouched upon the brambles.

The traditions and beliefs held about cats shown in this chapter seem at first sight to be tangled and conflicting, but actually one might say that they all point in one direction; they are evidence that cats were once regarded as sacred animals. In the same way the seasonal persecution of the wren in Celtic areas is a proof that it was once a sacred bird, just as the hatred of the yellow hammer in the Scottish Highlands is a sign that it was once sacred to the sun god. Christianity in its missionary days had to make its way against a profusely polytheistic mythology, with a good many blood sacrifices to abolish; and, though the missionaries managed to Christianize a good many holy days and sacred sites, and persuade converts to take some of the saints to their hearts, they seemed to have no alternative except to regard a number of the heathen gods as devils.

The dog had its place in ancient mythology, and some demon dogs have passed into folk tradition, but the dog had been too long a servant of man to lose its hold on his affection. The cat, loving though it could be, had retained a wildness and independence of its own, and when the witch-cult fever struck Europe it became easy for people to identify it with the witches. It has been the cat's tragedy.

6
Witches and their Familiars

There are many stories and traditions about witches and their cats, and these are of two kinds. The greater part of them were about shape-shifting witches which could take the form of cats, but some were about cats which were kept by lonely old women as pets, but were believed to be *familiars*, lesser devils given to the witches on their initiation by Satan, who acted as their servants, being sent by them on errands of mischief, to destroy cattle or to bring pining illnesses upon their enemies, but who became in the end their masters and gained control of their souls. We hear comparatively little about these familiars in the Continental witch trials where the chief emphasis is on the diabolic compact and witches' Sabbats, though we do find occasional traces of the belief, as in the legend of Dr Faustus and of the small brown dog which accompanied him as his familiar. In Scotland familiars more often take the form of a fairy or ghost, like Thom Reid, Betty Dunlop's familiar, who had been killed at the Battle of Pinkie, and who introduced her to the Fairies.[1]

In the English witch trials the judges were inclined to look for evidence on the Continental lines, of gatherings of witches, the Sabbats, the diabolic compact and Black Mass, but the evidence of the witches' neighbours was of familiars, of evil spells wrought upon children and cattle, of the evil eye, of fore-speaking. In the beginning of James I's reign Samuel Harsnett in his exposure of the popular superstition, well describes the kind of person who was likely to be suspected of being a witch:

> Out of these there is shaped the true *Idaea* of Witch, an olde weather-beaten Croane, having her Chinne and her knees meeting for age, walking like a bow leaning on a shaft, hollow-eyed, untoothed, furrowed on her face, having her lips trembling with the palsie, going mumbling in the streetes, one that hath forgotten her *pater noster*, and hath yet a shrewd tongue in her head, to call a drab, a drab.[2]

Such poor old creatures, at odds with their neighbours and the world, were those that were most often suspected of witchcraft, and those who in their loneliness were most likely to dote upon their pets, dogs and cats if they could afford them, if not, cheaper pets, such as rats, mice or toads.

Traditionally a black cat is the witch's favourite familiar. So much was this so that Enid Porter records in *The Folklore of East Anglia* that early in the nineteenth century an old woman was thrown into a pit near Monk Soham in Suffolk because she had a pet cat, and so she must be a witch. The only other piece of evidence against her was that she went to church in a black silk dress, therefore her means must be ill-gotten.[3]

In the earlier books on witchcraft and the earlier accounts of witch trials the familiar devils are a most miscellaneous company. In George Gifford's *Dialogue Concerning Witches* he says:

> The witches have their spirits, some hath one, some hath more, as two, three, foure or five, some in one likenesses, some in another, as like cattes, weasils, toads, or mise, whome they nourish with milk, or with a chicken, or by letting them sucke now and then a drop of blood.[4]

In the illustrations drawn by Miles Gales, the Vicar of Keighley, to Edward Fairfax's manuscript, *A Discourse of Witchcraft*, written to defend his children from an accusation of trickery and malice, there is an unusual variety of familiars supposed to be employed by the witches. In 1621 Edward Fairfax had brought six women from the Forest of Knaresborough to trial at the York Assizes,

accusing them of bewitching his daughters. There had been an outbreak among the children of one of those strange attacks of hysteria which had already brought many people to their deaths. The Knaresborough women were more fortunate than most, for the court dismissed the case against them, and the children were rather roughly handled. It was a case of what was called 'spectral evidence', and the Fairfax children were unusually imaginative. In one picture the familiars were three Lilliputian sheep, three dragon-like creatures, three fishes, a goat, a seal, a monkey, a kind of lizard and a pig. In another there were two cats, a winged devil carrying a woman, a human figure with a dog's head and eight birds of very various kinds. The cats form a small proportion of the company.[5]

The notorious Matthew Hopkins, the Witchfinder, in his pamphlet, *The Discovery of Witches*, claims to have seen some of the witches' familiars, not quite as fantastic as those seen by the Fairfax children. He said he had seen the six spirits of Elizabeth Clark, whom he watched for four nights, though he only named five. They were Holt, a white kitling, Jamara, a fat spaniel, without any legs at all, Vinegar Tom, the most fantastic of them, who was like a long-legged greyhound with a head like an ox, broad eyes and a long tail, Sacke-and-sugar, like a black rabbit,

and a polecat called Newes. On the same occasion another of the witches broke down and told him the names of her familiars, who had more fantastic names – Ilemanzer, Pecke-in-the-Crowne, Pyewackett, and Grizell-Greediguts.[6] Ursula Kempe, at the St Osyth witch trials of 1582, confessed to four imps, a grey tom cat called Tittey, a black one called Jack, a black toad called Pigin and a black lamb called Tyffin. The first two killed her enemies and the others caused illnesses and bodily harm to people who offended her.[7] There were some who, as Gifford said, had only one. Mother Sawyer, the Witch of Edmonton, had only one devil, a black dog,[8] and, according to the evidence of her little daughter Jennet, Elizabeth Device of Pendle had a dog too, a brown dog called Ball, which she sent out to kill John Robinson of Barley.[9]

These pet animals and the witch marks they made were a particular feature of the rural witch trials in England. It seems like an ironic comment on the English fondness for pets, but perhaps it is partly due to the extreme poverty and unattractiveness of most of the English suspects. The careful description of five of the suspected witches in Edward Fairfax's pamphlet gives one a fair picture of the average type of suspect.

The first is called Margaret Waite, a widow that some years ago came to dwell in these parts, with a husband, who brought with them an evil report for witchcraft and theft. The man died by the hand of the executioner for stealing, and his relict has increased the report she brought with her for witchery. Her spirit is a deformed thing with many feet, black of colour, rough with hair, the bigness of a cat, the name of it unknown.

The next is her daughter . . . . Her spirit is a white cat, spotted black and named Inges.

The third is Jennet Dibble, a very old widow, reputed a

witch for many years; and a constant report affirmeth that her mother, two aunts, two sisters, her husband and some of her children, have all been long esteemed Witches, so that it seemeth hereditary to her family. Her spirit is a great black cat, called Gibbe, which hath attended her for above forty year.

These are made up to a messe by Margaret Thorpe, daughter of Jennet Dibble. Her familiar is a bird, yellow in colour, about the bigness of a crow; the name of it is Tewit.

The fifth is Isobel Fletcher . . . a woman notoriously famed for a Witch, who had so powerful a hand over the wealthiest neighbours about her, that none of them dared to refuse to do anything that she required.[10]

Fairfax says that there was a sixth witch but does not seem to know anything about her. It is a strange, assorted collection of familiars; the two cats are the only natural creatures in it, and even Gibbe seems to have had an unnatural longevity.

Another cat who was rather long-lived, though he was said to have experienced some transformations, is to be found in one of the earliest of the Elizabethan witchcraft trials, that of the Chelmsford Witches in 1566. This was Sathan, who belonged to Elizabeth Francis, whose deposition has survived, though not the wording of the actual indictment.

She first learned this art of Witchcraft at the age of twelve years from her grandmother, whose name (was) Mother Eve of Hatfield Peverill, deceased.

Item: When she taught it to her, she counselled her to renounce God and his word, and to give of her blood to Sathan (as she termed it), which she delivered her in the likeness of a white spotted cat, and taught her to feed the said cat with bread and milk. And she did so. Also she taught her to call it by the name of Sathan and to keep it in a basket.

When this Mother Eve had given her the cat Sathan, then this Elizabeth desired of the said cat (calling it Sathan) that she might be rich and have goods. And he promised her she should, asking her what she would have. And she said sheep (for this cat spoke to her, as she confessed, in a strange hollow voice, but such as she understood by use). And this cat brought sheep into her pasture, black and white, which continued with her for a time, but in the end did all wear away, she knew not how.

Item: when she had gotten these sheep, she desired to have one Andrew Byles to be her husband, which was a man of some wealth; and the cat did promise she should, but that she must first consent that this Andrew should abuse her, and she so did.

And after, when this Andrew had abused her, he would not marry her. Wherefore she willed Sathan to waste his goods, which he forthwith did. And yet not being contented with this, she desired him to touch his body, which he forthwith did, whereof he died.

After this the story went on for some time. Elizabeth Francis looked out for another husband, and Sathan procured one for her, but they lived together with great unquietness, and she got Sathan to kill her baby at six months old, and when still her condition was no better she asked Sathan to lame her husband, which he did by creeping into his shoe in the form of a toad.

After she had had him for about fifteen years she wearied of her pet, and gave him to a neighbour, Agnes Waterhouse, in exchange for a cake, with full instructions for his treatment, as she had received them from her grandmother.

This relinquishment seems to have shifted the onus of guilt on to Mother Waterhouse, for, in spite of her confession to two murders, Elizabeth Francis was only sentenced to a year's imprisonment and Agnes Waterhouse was hanged. Sathan rather disappeared from the story in his cat form, for Mother Waterhouse was so anxious to use the wool that lined his basket that she changed him into a toad. This appears to have been his alternative form, according to Elizabeth Francis in her strange confession.[11]

This was an early trial. One that was probably the last of all was that of Jane Wenham at Hertford in 1712. Here again we have it assumed that cats are the natural familiars for a witch. Christina Hole, in *A Mirror of Witchcraft* gives an extract from the reports of the trial which lays stress upon the cats that surrounded her.

> It was taken notice of that a dismal Noise of Cats was at the Time, and several Times after, heard about the house, some Times their Cry resembling that of Young Children, at other Times they made a Hellish Noise, to which nothing can be resembled, this was accompanied by Scratchings heard by all that were in the House, under the Windows and at the Doors . . . . Several People saw these Cats, sometimes three or four in a company, which would run to Jane Wenham's House whenever anybody came up to them.[12]

This trial caused a great deal of controversy and was the occasion which roused Francis Hutchinson to write the book, *An Historical Essay Concerning Witchcraft*, published in 1718, which struck the last blow in the battle to defend helpless old women from the terrible sufferings which an accusation of witchcraft brought upon them.[13] The first blow had been struck by Reginald Scot in 1584, and he had been stirred by the St Osyth trials as Hutchinson had been by the trial of Jane Wenham. Educated men were convinced, but the countrymen were still bitter against witches. Jane Wenham in the end owed her life to Chief Justice Powell, who was in charge of the case. He obviously disbelieved in the accusation, and when, in spite of his direction, the jury brought her in as guilty he gave a formal sentence, but took pains to see that she was pardoned, and afterwards properly cared for. According to Wallace Notestein this was the last trial for witchcraft in England, and in 1736 the statute was repealed.[14]

When the crime of witchcraft was removed from the Statute Book the belief in it went underground and still persisted among those people whose culture lay chiefly in oral tradition.

After the trials ceased the waking and walking of witches to detect visits of their familiars ceased too. In the time when these cruel methods were practised the only living things that could have access to the suspects were often spiders and flies, and these were sometimes supposed to be the forms in which the witches' imps visited them. Afterwards people ceased to think of flies as possible familiars, and attention was focused on something larger. Toads remained first favourites in some parts of the country, but dogs and cats were high in the lists. Men as a whole had an affection for dogs, so they began to concentrate on cats. A north country anecdote of how a witch avenged her cat is told in *Folklore of the Lake District* by Marjorie Rawling.

Mary Baynes, who lived in Tebay early in the nineteenth century, had some reputation as a witch. Like Mother Shipton and Michael Scott she dealt in prophecies. One that was remembered was that fiery carriages without horses would one day rush up the dale above the Lune, and this stuck in men's memory until it was fulfilled, for in the 1840s, within a generation of her death, the railway was built over that route. Mary Baynes was ugly and crabbed, and was generally feared as a witch. Ned Sisson, the landlord of the Cross Keys at that time, had a dog, which one day killed Mary Baynes's pet cat, and he told his servant, Willan, to bury it. When the grave was dug Mary brought out the cat's body, and, giving Willan a book, she asked him to read some verses out of it. Willan was a rude, unfeeling man and he gave a great guffaw and tossed the cat's body into the hole, shouting:

> Ashes to ashes, dust to dust,
> Here's a hole, and go thou must!

Mary was justly and bitterly angry and cried out that he would be punished for this ribaldry. A few days later when he was ploughing, the share caught in a rock, and one of the handles glanced straight up into his face and blinded him. All the village believed that Mary Baynes had laid a spell on it, and they may well have thought that Ned Sisson was lucky to have got off scot-free. Mary was more shunned and feared than ever, but it may be that she was treated with more respect.[15]

Many of the later witchcraft stories turned on the curses laid by a witch on those who killed or ill-used her pet animals. Several of those told by W. H. Barrett in *More Tales from the Fens* contain this motif. There is, for instance, the story of 'Mother Kemp'. Old Mother Kemp lived in a half-ruined shack at the end of an old *drove*, or track-way through the Fens that led nowhere in particular. She had buried five husbands already, and was about to wed a sixth when he fell into one of the drains and was sucked into the pump that worked it. The man who lived in the pump-house discovered the body some days later, and told Mother Kemp that her sixth husband had died sooner than she expected. She yelled out curses on him so loud and so lurid that the men working in the fields near heard them and were much impressed. A short time after the pumping engine blew up as he was working on it, and he was killed. It was difficult to find anyone to take his place, as she had put a comprehensive curse on the engine as well, and at length the company put a stranger from a distance into the job, and gave him an old barge to live in. He had not been long there before the stove in the cabin exploded, and he was burned to death. After this old Mother Kemp was almost as much feared as she was hated. She lived alone, therefore, in her shack, with some two dozen cats and two snakes. There were several dairy farms around, and every morning one or other of the farmers would find one of his cows milked dry.

One night four young farmers who had been at a wedding celebration and ended up at a pub inspirited each other to go and have a look at Mother Kemp. They crept up to her shack, and peered in at the window. They saw her sitting at her fire with her twenty-four cats around her, a dull enough domestic scene until she picked up a whistle and began to play on it. Then she walked to the cupboard and let out two great snakes, who danced to the tune she played. Presently she put some powder on the fire, which burst into a blue flame, to which she made obeisance. After this she picked up a pail and came out of the cottage, accompanied by all the cats and the two snakes. The hiding watchers saw her making towards the pastures of Jowler Farm. One of the four spies was Jowler's son, and he ran back to his father's farm, told him to dress and bring his gun with him. Old Jowler let the bull out of his shed and loosed him in the pastures. The bull put

Mother Kemp to flight, and she raced towards the gate where the farmers were waiting, with the cats well in front of her and the bull close behind. When the cats got within range old Jowler fired, and killed two. The rest raced back towards the drain, which was too deep and swift for them to cross, followed by Mother Kemp. The bull lost interest and went back to the cows. When it was fully light Jowler took the cows back for milking, and when the milking was over he returned to the meadow, and shot twenty-three cats.

After that Old Mother Kemp would come night after night to the farm and stand pointing at it and yelling the most blood-curdling curses, until they could stand it no longer, and went into the town to complain of her, and a doctor and two magistrates came and fetched her away. Her shack was so much infested with vermin that its owner set fire to it one night, and it burned with great blue flames. That night old Mother Kemp died, but the curses she had left behind her fell on the farm. First Old Jowler's wife and daughter died, and one after another his stock died too. Then Jowler fell off a corn-stack and broke his neck, and young Jowler went to America and never came back again. The ill luck still clung to the farm. It was sold four times in six years, and at last it was left to go back to the Fen, and the sedge and weeds came back and the dykes were blocked, and the only thing left to show that men had once lived there was a tangle of blackthorn and a patch of nettles where Mother Kemp's shack once stood.[16]

'Spinning Jenny' is an even grimmer tale. It is about an old woman who made pets of the jackdaws and pigeons who nested round her cottage and of a dozen cats who shared her bed. She was generally reputed a witch and was much feared. A very brief summary will make the point. The tragedy started when the squire's lady was driving through the village wearing a large hat adorned with artificial cherries. Spinning Jenny was standing at her cottage door with one of the jackdaws on her shoulder. The jackdaw mistook the cherries for real ones and made a sudden

assault on them. The squire's lady was terrified, the coachman lashed Jenny with his whip and drove back to the Manor with the half-swooning lady inside. When the squire heard of it he ordered his gamekeeper to go and shoot all Jenny's jackdaws, but the keeper was afraid to do so, so the squire went down instead, with his dog and his gun. At the first shot the old witch came out with all her cats about her. The dog went for the largest cat and killed it, and the squire shot the rest, when he had finished off the jackdaws. Jenny cursed the dog and the squire and all who were concerned in the matter. The dog went mad, and escaped into the woods where he ran wild. In the end, after many misfortunes, the squire, the coachman and the keeper all committed suicide and the manor fell into ruins. The witch was finally destroyed by the dog, which was found strangled by his own chain.[17]

This is a terrible story, told with Barrett's characteristic grim zest and macabre humour. It will be seen, however, that cats have become the chief companions of witches in modern folklore. This is perhaps specially true of the eastern counties, where the witch trials were rampant. In the west the belief in familiars seems less common, and most witches are supposed to have had a more direct contact with the devil. The wicked Black Witch of Fraddam, however, is supposed to have ridden a huge black cat through the air, when she went to look for poisons and magical herbs.[18] In Somerset toads are perhaps commoner than cats as familiars, and people often say 'He's Tudded' when they mean 'He's bewitched'. However, in common tradition all over the country it is hard to separate the witch from her black cat.

7

Shape-Shifters

As we have seen, the witches' pet cats were generally regarded as her familiars, devils or imps in the form of cats, but it was equally common to suspect any cat seen entering a witch's house of being the witch herself. A witch was commonly credited with the power of shape-shifting, of assuming any form she chose, except of course that of a dove or a lamb, for these were sacred creatures. This power was rather a dangerous one to exercise, for any injury done to the witch in her animal form was suffered in her human body as well, though that might be sitting by the fireside or lying in bed, apparently asleep or in a trance; people were readier to attack and damage an animal than a human being and therefore witches were more at risk in animal form. A common story, of which we have an example given by Henderson from Thorpe's *Popular Tales and Traditions*, is that of a man attacked by a posse of cats who protects himself with his sword and cuts off a cat's paw, which he puts in his pocket. In the morning he finds a beautiful hand, with rings on it, in his pocket instead of the paw. He recognizes the rings as belonging to a neighbour's wife.[1] Heywood uses this tale as a piece of decoration in his play, *The Late Lancashire Witches*. This was written and produced during the trial of the witches in 1634, and the epilogue leaves the matter in the air. What Heywood half-prophesied actually took place. The jury condemned seventeen of the accused suspects but the judge was sceptical and suspended sentence, and in the end the accusation of the Robinson boy, on which the case

turned, was found to be a piece of pure invention, and the accused were acquitted, though some of them had died in prison in the meantime.[2]

William Henderson in *Folk-Lore of the Northern Counties* gives a story, Auld Betty of Halifax, told him by a local schoolmaster, of damage done to a witch in cat form.

An old man whom I knew well in my boyhood, was said to have undertaken the dangerous task of catching this witch, and drawing blood from her. Armed with a three-pronged table-fork he stationed himself beside the fire in the house where she was suspected of doing mischief by night in the shape of a black cat. According to the directions for the capture of witches, he had a cake baking before the fire. All at once he perceived a huge black cat sitting by the fire washing its face, though he had not seen or heard it come in. 'Cake burns,' cried the cat. 'Turn it then,' replied the witch-catcher. 'Cake burns,' it said once more, and he made the same answer again and again. The man had been specially charged on no account to mention any holy name while watching the cat, and for a long time he remembered this, but, worn out with watching, and worried by the continued cry of 'Cake burns,' he lost his temper, and answered with an imprecation. Instantly the cat sprang up the chimney, and after it scrambled the witch-catcher, trying to pierce it with the three-pronged fork. This he accomplished at last, but not till he had been dreadfully scratched by his antagonist. The next day the old witch-woman was ill in bed, and continued there for some days, but the person who had been witched was relieved.[3]

Another story told by Henderson is of a Yorkshireman who had often lost his young piglets, and suspected a cat which he had seen prowling about the place. He went for advice to the Wise Man of Stokesley, who told him that they were bewitched by an old woman who lived near. He watched for the cat, armed with the poker, and when she appeared, flung it at her. The cat disappeared, and they found the old woman next morning with a broken leg. This was felt to be conclusive.[4]

A version of the same story is told in Wales. It was one of the exploits of Huw Llwyd, a seventh son of a seventh son and skilled in magic. There was an inn near Bettws-y-Coed where travellers were often robbed, however carefully they locked their doors. Huw Llwyd determined to put an end to these practices, so he went to stop the night there, assuming the character of an English army officer. The two attractive sisters who kept the inn made themselves very agreeable to him and told a number of anecdotes of travel in places which he had never visited. When it came to bedtime he said that it was his custom to sleep with lights burning and had enough candles brought to the room to last him for the night. He locked his door, undressed and left his clothes near his bed, and took his sword to bed with him, convenient to his hand. After a while two black cats came down the chimney and began playing about the room, getting nearer and nearer to the bed. Huw seemed to be sound asleep. At last the cats began to play about with his clothes, and one put her paw in the pocket where he kept his purse. Like a flash Huw sat up in bed, pulled out his sword and cut at the thieving paw. There was a terrible howl and both cats shot up the chimney. In the morning only one of the sisters came to serve breakfast, and when Huw enquired about the other she said that her sister was ill. After the meal Huw said he must go, but he insisted on seeing the other sister whose company

he had enjoyed so much the night before. In spite of resistance he got his way, cordially condoled with his hostess and held out his hand to wish her goodbye. She held out her left hand. 'Oh no!' he said laughing, 'I never took a left hand in my life. Give me the other.' She drew the other out from under the bedclothes, and it was heavily bandaged. Then he was sure of what had happened. 'So this is the little paw that was in my pocket!' he said. 'Well, I have drawn your power to hurt me, and I will make sure of the other.' So he caught her sister's hand, drew out his knife and cut it so that the blood ran freely. And from that time on, though the two sisters kept the inn, there were no more thefts, for their witch powers had gone with the blood-letting.[5]

A Highland legend on the same theme is given in *A Forgotten Heritage* by Hannah Arthur. It is about a witch called Maggie Osborne, who probably had a small farm, as she was rich enough to employ a maidservant.

> On another occasion she quarrelled with her maid, and forced her to brew by night. About midnight some cats leaped into the brew house and began to fight. One sprang suddenly on the girl and tried to push her into a cooler filled with boiling water, but she snatched a ladle and scalded the cat instead. In the morning Maggie was found with a blistered back.[6]

Isobel Gowdie of Auldearn in Scotland, who made a remarkable voluntary confession of witchcraft in 1662, gives very explicit accounts of shape-shifting and the formula by which it was effected. Like many country witches she most commonly turned herself into a hare, but she sometimes took the form of a large crow, and occasionally made herself into a cat though this seemed to have been done more for recreation than for any practical purpose. She gives the cat formula as

> I shall go intil a cat
> With sorrow and sych and a black shot
> And I shall go in the Devil's name
> Ay while I come home again.

And she adds:

When we would be in the shape of cats we did nothing but cry and wrow (caterwaul), and riving, and as it were, worrying on one another; and when we come to our own shapes again, we will find the scratches and rives on our own skin very sore.

If we, in the shape of a cat, a hare, or any other likenesses, go to any of our neighbour's houses, being witches, we will say

'I conjure thee,
Go with me.'

and presently they become as we are, either cats, hares, crows etc. and go with us whither we would.[7]

Another typical example of witches being injured in their animal form is quoted by Jacqueline Simpson from *The Sussex County Magazine* of 1935. In a collection of the beliefs of a countryman named Tom Reed that a friend of his called Crowhurst had once caught an animal in the dark in the garden of a house that was supposed to be witch-haunted, and when he called for a light to see what he was holding there was nothing in his hands. On another occasion, however, he shot a cat in the leg which was always roaming round the house whenever his wife was out. On that occasion she came limping back from market saying she had had a fall.[8]

There are many more instances of this belief, some about cats and some about hares and toads, but this sample is enough to show that the witch could not play her pranks except at considerable risk.

In the seventeenth century the common people believed that witches could turn casually into animals and back again. We find an account of such a power in *Dr. Lamb's Darling*, a pamphlet published in 1653, which gave an account of the trial of Anne Bodenham before Baron Wilde. This piece of evidence is given by a maid sent to fetch malefic implements from her.

Yet before she departed, the witch desired the maid to live with her, and she would teach her a more stranger Art: What's that, said the maid, she answered You shall know presently, and forthwith she appeared in the shape of a great black Cat, and lay along by the chimney: at which the maid was affrighted, she came into her shape again.[9]

The belief that witches can take the form of cats is widespread in Europe and occurs throughout the world. In *Folk-Tales of the Magyars* we are told that witches take the form of black cats.[10] In *Uncle Remus* by Joel Chandler Harris, Chapter 31 is devoted to 'A Plantation Witch'. The little boy one evening finds Old Uncle Remus has found 'witch-stirrup' in the mane of his master's pony. It is witches he suspects, not elves. The boys asks him to describe witches, but he hardly feels equal to the task. 'Conjun folk' can tell a witch the minute they see one, but it is more difficult for ordinary people. Still he can tell a clear case when he sees it. 'I ain't bin useter no conjun myse'f, but I bin livin' long nuff fer ter know w'en you meets up wid a big black cat in de middle er de road, wid yaller eyeballs, dars yo' witch fresh fum de Ole Boy.' Uncle Remus goes on to tell of a friend on the plantation who suspected his brother was a witch and a shape-shifter, and after a number of tricks had been played he determined to watch. Sure enough, at midnight his brother peeled his skin right off and flew out of the cabin in the shape of a bat. The man went over to the skin and put a big handful of salt inside it. Then he lay down on the bed and watched. Presently a big black cat stole in and went towards the bed, but the man drove her away. Next a big black dog came and he threw a big block of wood at it and it ran. Then a screech-owl flew in and perched on the rafters, but the man pulled a red-hot shovel out of the fire and scared it off. The last creature that came was a great black wolf with fiery eyes who seized the skin and made off with it. I daresay the witch-brother thought he'd won the match that time, but in about two minutes a dreadful hollering and yelling broke out, so the man lit a lantern and went to see what was happening, and there was his brother grovelling and rolling about in the grass with salt inside his skin burning like fire, for no witch can endure salt. Next morning he could hobble about in a kind of way, but that was the end of his witchery, and the whole settlement was free of witchcraft after that.[11]
Grant Stewart in his *Popular Superstitions of the Highlands of Scotland* considers that the hare is the witch's first choice as a convenient form to take, the second is a cat, the third, strangely

enough, is a stone in which shape she wedges herself between the sock and coulter of a plough and is a considerable hindrance to ploughing, and the fourth is the form of a bird, generally a raven, but sometimes a magpie.[12] Grant Stewart gives two vivid examples of the use of the cat form in malevolent attacks upon her victims. The two tales are linked together, so that they almost form one tale.

The first is the account of the death of John Macgillichallum of Razay who was much admired for his talents, and high courage and generally approved as the active and inexorable enemy of the witches, who were much dreaded in the Highlands. Naturally this trait did not endear him to the local witches. The best thing that could happen as far as they were concerned was that he should be destroyed. It was not long before he gave them an opportunity.

One fine day Razay set out to the Isle of Lewes to hunt the deer that were abundant there. He took his followers with him, the flower of the young men of Razay. It was a beautiful day and the sport was admirable. It had never been so good, and they hunted till sunset and spent the evening in great merriment in their hunting lodge, dining off roasted venison and good whisky, with songs and music and tales, until late into the night. But while they were sleeping the wind got up, and they wakened to a squally and blusterous day. Razay was anxious to get home and ordered the crew to prepare the boat. Many of them were doubtful whether the crossing was possible, but danger was a spur to their laird, so he led them all down to the jetty, but many of them were still doubtful, so Razay broached a keg of whisky, and their spirits began to rise, though several were still doubtful. Whilst they were debating an old crone hobbled up to them, and Razay appealed to her as bound to know the place. 'Ay, ay,' said she, 'I've been here this eighty year, and it's as smooth as the back of your hand in comparison to the days when my father would cross the water; aye and my husband too and my young son, and come back as safe as if they were rocking in their cradle. But they've no seamanship these days and are feared if the wind gives but a wee whistle. I've aye heard tell that Razay's lads are the greatest cowards in all Scotland, and I can see it's true the day.'

At that taunt the most cautious man among them would not have held back for the wealth of the Indies. They pushed out from the jetty, and hoisted sail, and the wind caught them and whirled them out to sea, while the storm doubled and trebled itself, with lightning and thunder and torrents of rain, so that there was no putting in to shore again. Razay kept up his brave heart and made his way to the tiller, and the hearts of his crew began to rise as he kept her head steadily to point of Aird on Skye. They had almost begun to hope when a great black cat crawled up on to the boat and began to climb the mast. Another came and another until they covered the rigging and blackened all the lee side of the boat. Last came an enormous beast and climbed the main mast. Razay called out to the crew to kill it, but as they made towards it all the cats with one movement heeled over the boat, and every man on board was engulfed in the sea and was drowned.[13]

On that very day one of Razay's greatest friends, so keen a sportsman that he was generally called the Hunter of the Hills and, like him a determined enemy of the witches, was warming himself in his hunting lodge in the forest of Gaich, in Badenoch, listening to the howling of the storm outside. His two dogs lay stretched by the fire at his side and his gun was propped up in the corner of the bothy. As he sat, half-dozing, the door opened by a narrow crack and a poor, miserable, drenched cat stole into the room. The dogs bounded up, their hackles rising, and made for the creature, but to his surprise, she spoke with a human voice. 'Oh, great Hunter of the Hills,' she said, 'I appeal to you for protection. I know your hatred of my kind, but spare a poor jaded wretch, who flies to you for protection from the cruelty of her sisterhood!'

The Hunter was touched. Though from her speech he judged her to be a witch, yet he was too generous to oppress an enemy brought so low. He made his dogs lie down, and told her that she might sit by the fire and dry herself. But she held back and shivered. 'Your dogs are still angry', she said, 'I am afraid they will tear me to pieces. I have a long hair here. I pray you to put it round them and bind them together.' The Hunter became still more suspicious. He took the strange, long hair and pretended to tie the dogs, but he put it round one of the rafters of the bothy; and the cat stole in and sat by the fire. Presently the Hunter noticed that the cat was growing larger and larger.

'A bad death to you, you nasty beast,' he said laughing, 'you are getting very large.'

'Aye, aye,' said the cat, chuckling too. 'My featheries are swelling as they dry.'

The Hunter said nothing, but watched the cat, who continued to grow larger and larger till suddenly he saw the Goodwife of Laggan sitting in front of him.

'Now, Hunter of the Hills,' she said, 'your hour of reckoning is at hand. You and Macgillichallum of Razay were the greatest enemies of my devoted sisterhood. We have reckoned with Razay. He lies a lifeless corpse at the bottom of the sea. And now, Hunter of the Hills, it is your turn.' And at that she seemed to enlarge yet more terribly and to grow as ugly as a devil, and sprang at him. But the dogs were not bound by the hair and they sprang to defend their master. They fastened on the witch's breasts, she tried to escape from them, shrieking loudly: 'Fasten hair! Fasten!', for she fancied that the hair was wound round the dogs. The hair fastened until the two rafters round which the Hunter had thrown it snapped like matchwood, but still the dogs tore at the witch, who dragged them with her out of the house and did not let go till she had torn every tooth out of their heads. When she got loose she flew away as a raven. Her wailing died away and the dogs crawled back to their master, and as he stroked and praised them they licked his hands and died. The Hunter wept over them as if they had been his own children. Then he buried them and went sadly home. His wife was out, and he waited sometime till she got back. 'Where have you been, my love?' he said. 'On a sad errand,' she replied, 'I have been to visit the Goodwife of Laggan, who has been struck by a sudden illness, and is not expected to live through the night. All the neighbours are with her.' 'That's sad hearing,' said her husband. 'What is it ails the worthy woman?' 'It seems she was out on the moss cutting peats and the storm came down, so that she was soaked through, and was struck with a sudden colic.' 'It is only fitting that I should go to see her', said the Hunter. 'Let us have dinner quickly and go.'

They soon reached the room, where all the neighbours were surrounding her bed, mourning the sufferings of one whom they had always regarded as a good neighbour and a worthy woman. The Hunter made his way through the crowd and stripped back the blankets so that they all could see the marks of the dogs' teeth on her breasts and arms. 'Look at this vile witch!' he said. 'This very day she compassed the death of Macgillichallum of Razay and tried to murder me.' And he told the whole story of what had happened. Everyone there was both amazed and convinced, for the marks of the dogs' teeth were plain on her body. All were prepared to drag her out and execute her without further trial, but the old witch pled with them to spare her human vengeance, for terrible sufferings awaited her from the fiend who had cheated and allured her, and who was now mocking at her torments. 'Take warning from me,' she said, 'and have no traffic with Master whom I have served so long.' And she went on to tell them the whole story of her apprenticeship to evil and of all the terrible things she had done, ending with the account of the death of Razay and the foiled attempt upon his friend. And when she had told all she died.

That same night one of her neighbours was returning home from Strathdearn and just entering the dreary forest of Monalea in Badenoch, when he met a woman dressed in black, running at a great speed, and as she approached him she asked him how far it was from the kirkyard of Dalarossie, and if she could reach it before twelve o'clock. He said he thought that she could if she continued at that pace. She sped on, lamenting as she ran. He had not gone many miles when he met a great black dog, snuffing along the track, and shortly after he met another. Shortly after him there was a strong black man on a fine, fleet black courser, who paused to ask him if he had seen a woman going that way. He replied that he had, running very fast. 'And were there two black dogs after her?' said the black stranger. 'There were,' said the traveller, 'Two great dogs.' 'And do you think that the dogs will overtake her before she reaches the kirkyard of Dalarossie?' 'They should at any rate be hard on her heels,' said the traveller. With that the stranger gathered his reins and galloped away, and the traveller hurried towards home, for it was an uncanny encounter in an uncanny place. He had not gone far however when the black rider overtook him with the woman across his saddle bow and two dogs hanging one on her breast and one on her thigh. 'Where did you overtake her?' asked the traveller. 'Just as she was entering the kirkyard of Dalarossie,' said the black huntsman, and galloped away.

When the traveller got home and heard the story of the witch of Laggan he had no doubt that the woman in black was the soul of the witch flying for protection from the demons to whom she had sold herself to the kirkyard of Dalarossie, which is so sacred a place that any witch who visits it, dead or alive, is freed from her contract with Satan.[14]

This grim story shows the great terror of witchcraft felt in the Highlands of Scotland in the seventeenth and eighteenth centuries. The story of the Black Huntsman will remind those who know anything of Scandinavian folklore of the legend of Odin's pursuit of the harmless little woodwives.[15]

There is no doubt that these Highlanders believed in the witches' power of shape–shifting, and that they believed that their most sinister appearance was in the form of cats. And it was not the Highlanders alone who held that belief. In Richard Chase's *Grandfather Tales* there is an unusual version of 'Hop o' my Thumb' in which the Giant's place is taken by an old witch who, with her whole coven, can turn into a swarm of cats.

The Two Lost Babes

One time there was a man and a woman come from England
to the United States – back when this country was first settlin'
up and families was scattered about in the wilderness. This
man and his wife they had two children named Buck and
Bess, and they lived 'way back in the mountains where it was
solid woods. They had one little patch cleared for corn and
beans but they had to live mostly off of wild game, and
game had got so scarce they was about to starve. And one
night the old woman started in talkin' to the old man, told
him she didn't see how they could make out having two
children to feed, said he ought to take 'em off and lose 'em in
the wilderness – let 'em make out the best they could. So
they decided to take Buck and Bess off the next day and leave
'em somewhere in the woods. Buck he had stayed awake and
heard every word they said, so he slipped out just about
daylight and picked up little white flint rocks till his pockets
was full.

Well, that mornin' the man took Buck and Bess 'way off
in the wilderness and when they got a right long ways off
from the house they come to a chestnut grove and he told the
children to stay there and pick up chestnuts while he hunted
some game. Left 'em there and pulled out. But Buck he told
Bess, says, 'Come on. No use in us waitin'.' Buck he had
dropped them rocks on the way. So he commenced followin'
his trail of white flints and he and Bess got back in home
about dark. The man told 'em, says, 'Why, we was jest fixin'
to start to hunt for ye. You must 'a not stayed where I told
you to. We thought you was lost.'

So the next mornin' he got up real early and took the
children off 'fore daylight. So Buck didn't have no time to
pick up rocks but he pulled a couple of ears of corn, and hid
'em under his shirt-tail, and he 'uld shell off some grains
every few steps. That time they went about twice as far, and
then the old man left'em and pulled out. Buck he tried to
follow that trail of corn and he found it pretty well for about
a half a mile but the squirrels and coons and 'possums and
birds had come along and eat the corn. So that time the
children really was lost. They tried to beat their way back

99

but it got plumb thick dark. Bess she got awful scared 'cause they could hear the wolves howlin' and pan'ters screamin'. And then she give plumb out and Buck took her up on his back – told her not to cry, said he'd get her out all right.

Come to a big high rock-cliff after a while, cloomb up on it and saw a light off across the holler. Headed for where that light was at, come to a road and directly they found the house. Knocked on the door and an ugly-lookin' woman opened it. She told 'em to come on in. There was a boy there about Buck's size, named Cooklepea. So the old woman give the three children some mush and milk and sent 'em up in the loft. Bess she went on off to sleep, but Buck and Cooklepea they got to talkin' and Cooklepea told Buck the old woman was a witch. Said she killed all the travellers that came by there and the only reason she hadn't killed him was she had to have somebody to cut her firewood. Said he never could get away 'cause she had clip-boots that went a mile at a clip. So Cooklepea and Buck they made 'em a plan to try to get away. They slipped shingles out the roof 'till they had a hole big enough to get out of, and they laid back down and made like they was sleepin'.

The old woman she got out a big butcher knife and commenced whettin' it on her whet-rock. She whetted it a while, then she called Cooklepea, 'Cooklepea, you all asleep yet?'

'No'm.'

So she went on whettin' her knife – scrape, scrape, scrape.

Then Buck and Cooklepea tied the corner of one of them quilts to a rafter and put it out the hole and woke Bess up and helped her out that hole and down to the ground.

Scrape, scrape, scrape.

'Cooklepea, you all asleep yet?'

'Bess is, but Buck and me ain't.'

Scrape, scrape, scrape.

Then Buck and Cooklepea fixed the straw and the quilts so it looked like Buck and Bess was still there a-sleepin', and then Cooklepea helped Buck out and down to the ground.

Scrape, scrape, scrape.

'Cooklepea, you all asleep yet?'

'Bess is, and Buck is, but I ain't.'

Scrape, scrape, scrape.

Then Cooklepea he untied that quilt and fixed it so it looked like he was under it, and then he crawled out the hole and Buck and Bess helped him ease down to the ground. Then the three children they slipped off from there and when they got out in the road they run for life.

Scrape, scrape, scrape.

'Cooklepea, you all asleep yet?'

Scrape, scrape, scrape.

And when there didn't nobody answer, the old woman cloomb up in the loft and slashed her old butcher-knife into Buck's and Bess's quilts. Went on back down the ladder and went to sleep. And next mornin' she built up a big fire to cook the two children. Hollered for Cooklepea to get up and cut some more wood, and when he never answered she went up in the loft and jerked up Cooklepea's quilt. Then she jerked up them other two quilts, and she was mad as time! Back down the ladder she went, and grabbed up her clip-boots, and out the door. She smelled around and smelled around till she smelled which-a-way the three children had gone, then she jerked on her clip-boots.

Well, Buck and Bess and Cooklepea they was sharp. They run to that big old rock-cliff and Cooklepea showed 'em where there was a long cave-like place back up under that rock – just was big enough for them to crawl in, and couldn't no grown person get in at all. So they slipped in there and went 'way back, and waited, and listened.

And time the old woman had her clip-boots on she took one step and there she was on top of that rock-cliff. Then she took off her clip-boots and smelled around up there till she traced them kids to the mouth of that little cave, and she tried to get in but she couldn't. So she reached in her long old skinny arm but she couldn't reach 'em either.

'O yes,' she says, 'I'll jest wait for ye. You'll git hongry enough in a few days.'

So she went and laid down on top of that rock-cliff. Put her boots under her head and waited. She waited and waited, waited till about twelve but there wasn't a sound from them children, and the sun got good and warm and pretty soon the old woman went on off to sleep.

And when Buck and Bess and Cooklepea heard her snorin' they slipped up to the top of the rock-cliff, and Buck and Cooklepea give the old woman a quick shove and Bess she grabbed hold on them clip-boots. The old woman went rollin' and squallin' down that rock-cliff and landed in a briar thicket, and Bess handed Cooklepea the clip-boots right quick and when he got 'em on he grabbed Buck and Bess around the waist and lifted 'em up off the ground.

The old woman she'd done scrambled out the bresh and here she come a-tearin' back up the rock-cliff all scratched up and her hair full of leaves and trash, and she reached and made a grab for them children but 'fore she got there Cooklepea he took one step – and that put 'em a mile away from her.

So Cooklepea he held on to Buck and Bess and in about three more clips they landed in the lowland settle-ment. Then Cooklepea took the boots off and they went to the sheriff and told him all about that old woman killin' folks.

'You may be right,' he told 'em, 'but you got to have evidence. You got any evi-dence?'

Cooklepea told him anyhow he could prove the old woman was a witch; said he knew when she had her witch meetin's. Said she was the head of a big gang of witches. So he told when the next witch meetin' was appointed, and they waited till that night. Then Cooklepea lent the sheriff the clip–boots and he took Cooklepea up on his back and Cooklepea showed him which way to head with them clip–boots. He stepped out and in just a few clips there they was at the old woman's house. So they looked through a crack in the logs and listened to the witches. After a while they heard one of 'em say, 'Well, I've heard it told a woman never could keep a secret.'

'That ain't so,' says this old lady. 'I've kept a secret. I been killin' travelers that come through here; melted lead and poured it in their ears while they was asleep, and robbed 'em and cooked 'em and eat 'em and buried the bones. Yes, indeed; and that's a secret I've kept more'n thirty years.'

Well, the sheriff went and banged on the door and hollered.

And all kinds of black cats jumped out the door time he opened it. And when they went in the house there wasn't a soul in there – just one old black cat. Hit come sidlin' up to 'em right friendly-like but the sheriff he kicked it away and then it made for the door but Cooklepea already had the door shut. So then the sheriff hollered again and grabbed the black cat and shook it – and there was the old woman.

The sheriff arrested her and clipped on back to the settlement with her under one arm and Cooklepea under the other. And Buck and Bess and Cooklepea witnessed against

the old woman and the sheriff he testified, too; and that was evi-dence enough so they burnt that old witch the next day.

And Cooklepea and Bess got married, and him and Buck went to clearin' land, and Bess she kept house for both of 'em. And Bess and Cooklepea had twelve young 'uns and they all done well.[16]

Happily there were some other people who turned a kindlier eye on the cat.

8
Fairy Tales

People under Spells

Most of the tales and anecdotes that have been given so far have been legends, that is, they have been believed by the people who told them and are expected to be received as factual. When we come to fairytales, or *Märchen*, we are on different ground. These tales are frankly fictional, though they are generally founded on received beliefs. Hansel and Gretel, for instance, was undoubtedly first told when the belief in witchcraft was widespread and general, and when cannibalistic charges were brought against witches. The more primitive fairytales, though they did not pretend to be factual, were squarely founded on folk belief. When the French court adopted fairytales and made them fashionable, the tales were a good deal sophisticated, as were some of the fairy traditions. Those of Charles Perrault's were a reasonably close re-telling of the traditional tales, but other adaptors became more and more fantastical in their variations. The wide distribution of some of the stories is an indication of their status as old folktales. Perrault's 'Puss-in-Boots', for instance, might well be thought of as the offspring of Perrault's lively imagination but that variants are found all over Europe, in Africa, India and Indonesia and the West Indies.[1] In the French version there is no explanation of the cat's extraordinary powers, but in several variants the cat is an enchanted human, who is freed by decapitation. 'Lord Peter' from Norway is one example of this form. It is to be found in Dasent's *Tales from the Norse*. Stith Thompson considered that Dasent's version was too much adorned, but this is a fault which can be found in many of the earlier reports of folk tales, and this version seems on the whole a straightforward narrative, told in a direct, simple style.

Lord Peter

Once on a time there was a poor couple, and they had nothing in the world but three sons. What names the two elder had I can't say, but the youngest he was called Peter. So when their father and mother died, the sons were to share what was left, but there was nothing but a porridge-pot, a griddle and a cat.

The eldest, who was to have the first choice, he took the pot; 'for,' said he, 'whenever I lend the pot to any one to boil porridge, I can always get leave to scrape it.'

The second took the griddle; 'for,' said he, 'whenever I lend it to anyone, I'll always get a morsel of dough to make a bannock.'

But the youngest, he had no choice left him; if he was to choose anything it must be the cat.

'Well,' said he, 'if I lend the cat to anyone I can't get much by that; for if pussy gets a drop of milk, she'll want it all herself. Still, I'd best take her along with me; I shouldn't like her to go about here and starve.'

So the brothers went out into the world to try their luck, and each took his own way; but when the youngest had gone a while, the Cat said,

'Now you shall have a good turn, because you wouldn't let me stay behind in the old cottage and starve. Now, I'm off to the wood to lay hold of a fat head of game, and then you must go up to the King's palace that you see yonder, and say that you are come with a little present for the King; and when he asks who sends it, you must say, "Why, who should it be from but Lord Peter?"'

Well, Peter hadn't waited long before back came the Cat with a reindeer from the wood; she had jumped upon the reindeer's head, between his horns, and said, 'If you don't go straight to the king's palace I'll claw your eyes out.'

So the reindeer had to go whether he liked it or no. And when Peter got to the palace he went into the kitchen with

the deer, and said, 'Here I'm come with a little present for
the King, if he won't despise it.'

Then the King went into the kitchen, and when he saw the
fine plump reindeer, he was very glad.

'But, my dear friend,' he said, 'who in the world is it who
sends me such a fine gift?'

'Oh,' said Peter, 'who should send it but Lord Peter?'

'Lord Peter! Lord Peter!' said the King. 'Pray tell me where
he lives;' for he thought it a shame not to know so great a
man. But that was just what the lad wouldn't tell him; he
daren't do it, he said, because his master had forbidden him.

So the King gave him a good bit of money to drink his
health, and bade him be sure and say all kinds of pretty
things, and many thanks for the present to his master when
he got home.

Next day the Cat went again into the wood, jumped on a
red deer's head, and sat between his horns, and forced him to
go to the palace. Then Peter went again into the kitchen, and
said he was come with a little present for the King, if he
would be pleased to take it. And the King was still more
pleased to get the red deer than he had been to get the
reindeer, and asked again who it was that sent so fine a present.

'Why, it's Lord Peter of course,' said the lad, but when the
King wanted to know where Lord Peter lived, he got the
same answer as the day before, and this day, too, he gave
Peter a good lump of money to drink his health with.

The third day the Cat came with an elk. And so when
Peter got into the palace-kitchen, and said he had a little
present for the King, if he'd be pleased to take it, the King
came out at once into the kitchen; and when he saw the
grand big elk, he was so glad he scarce knew which leg to
stand on; and this day, too, he gave Peter many more
dollars – at least a hundred. He wished now, once for all, to
know where the Lord Peter lived, and asked and asked about
this thing and that, but the lad said he daren't say, for his
master's sake, who had strictly forbidden him to tell.

'Well then,' said the King, 'beg Lord Peter to come and see
me.'

Yes, the lad would take that message, but when Peter got

out into the yard again and met the Cat, he said:
'A pretty scrape you've got me into now, for here's the king,
who wants me to come and see him, and you know I've
nothing to go in but these rags I stand and walk in.'

'Oh, don't be afraid about that,' said the Cat; 'in three days
you shall have coach and horses, and fine clothes, so fine that
the gold falls from them, and then you may go and see the
king very well. But mind, whatever you see in the king's
palace, you must say you have far better and grander things of
your own. Don't forget that.'

No, no, Peter would bear that in mind, never fear.

So when three days were over the Cat came with a coach
and horses, and clothes and all that Peter wanted, and
altogether it was as grand as anything you ever set eyes on;
so off he set, and the Cat ran alongside the coach. The King
met him well and graciously; but whatever the King offered
him, and whatever he showed him, Peter said 'twas all very
well, but he had much finer and better things in his own
house. The King seemed not quite to believe this, but Peter
stuck to what he said, and at last the King got so angry, he
couldn't bear it any longer.

'Now I'll go home with you,' he said, 'and see if it be true
what you've been telling me, that you have far finer and
better things of your own. But if you've been telling a pack
of lies, Heaven help you, that's all I say.'

'Now you've got me into a fine scrape,' said Peter to the
Cat, 'for here's the King coming home with me; but my
home, that's not so easy to find, I think.'

'Oh! never mind,' said the Cat; 'only do you drive after me
as I run before.'

So off they set; first Peter, who drove after his Cat, and
then the King and all his court.

But when they had driven a good bit, they came to a great
flock of fine sheep, that had wool so long that it almost
touched the ground.

'If you'll only say;' said the Cat to the shepherd, 'this flock
of sheep belongs to Lord Peter, when the King asks you, I'll
give you this silver spoon,' which she had taken with her
from the King's palace.

Yes, he was willing enough to do that. So when the King came up, he said to the lad who watched the sheep:

'Well, I never saw so large and fine a flock of sheep in my life! Whose is it, my little lad?'

'Why,' said the lad, 'whose should it be but Lord Peter's?'

A little further on they came to a great, great herd of fine brindled kine, who were all so sleek the sun shone from them.

'If you'll only say,' said the Cat to the neat-herd, 'this herd is Lord Peter's, when the King asks you, I'll give you this silver ladle;' and the ladle too she had taken from the King's palace.

'Yes, with all my heart,' said the neat-herd.

So when the king came up, he was quite amazed at the fine fat herd, for such a herd he had never seen before, and so he asked the neat-herd who owned those brindled kine.

'Why, who should own them but Lord Peter?' said the neat-herd.

So they went on a little farther, and came to a great, great drove of horses, the finest you ever saw, six of each colour, bay and black and brown and chestnut.

'If you'll only say this drove of horses is Lord Peter's when the King asks you,' said the cat, 'I'll give you this silver goblet;' and the goblet too she had taken from the palace.

Yes, the lad was willing enough; and so when the King came up, he was quite amazed at the great drove of horses, for the match of those horses he had never yet set eyes on, he said.

So he asked the lad who watched them, whose all these blacks and bays and browns and chestnuts were.

'Whose should they be,' said the lad, 'but Lord Peter's?'

So when they had gone a good bit further they came to a castle; first there was a gate of tin, and next a gate of silver, and next a gate of gold. The castle itself was of silver, and so dazzling white, that it quite hurt one's eyes to look at the sunbeams which fell on it just as they reached it.

So they went into it, and the Cat told Peter to say this was his house. As for the castle inside, it was far finer than it looked outside, for everything was pure gold – chairs, and tables and benches, and all. And when the King had gone all over it, and seen everything high and low, he got quite shameful and downcast.

'Yes,' he said at last, 'Lord Peter, has everything far finer than I have, there's no gainsaying that.' And so he wanted to be off home again.

But Peter begged him to stay to supper, and the king stayed, but he was sour and surly the whole time.

So as they sat at supper, back came the Troll who owned the castle, and gave such a great knock at the door.

'WHO'S THIS EATING MY MEAT AND DRINKING MY MEAD LIKE SWINE IN HERE' roared out the Troll.

As soon as the Cat heard that she ran down to the gate.

'Stop a bit,' she said, 'and I'll tell you how the farmer set to work to get in his winter rye.'

And so she told him such a long story about the winter rye.

'First of all, you see, he plows his field, and then he dungs it, and then he plows it again, and then he harrows it;' and so she went on till the sun rose.

'Oh do look behind you, and there you'll see such a lovely lady,' said the Cat to the Troll.

So the Troll turned round, and, of course, as soon as he saw the sun he burst.

'Now all this is yours,' said the Cat to Lord Peter. 'Now you must cut off my head; that's all I ask for what I have done for you.'

'Nay, nay,' said Lord Peter, 'I'll never do any such thing. That's flat.'

'If you don't,' said the Cat, 'see if I don't claw your eyes out.'

Well, so Lord Peter had to do it, though it was sore against his will. He cut off the Cat's head, but there and then she became the loveliest princess you ever set eyes on, and Lord Peter fell in love with her at once.

'Yes, all this greatness was mine first,' said the princess, 'but a Troll bewitched me to be a Cat in your father's and mother's cottage. Now you may do as you please, whether you take me to your queen or not, for you are now King over all this realm.'

Well, well, there was little doubt Lord Peter would be willing enough to have her as his queen, and so there was a wedding that lasted eight whole days, and a feast besides, and after it was over I stayed no longer with Lord Peter and his lovely queen, and so I can't say anything more about them.[2]

Peter had chosen, or been chosen by, a rather unscrupulous lady, but he was not over-loaded with scruples himself, though his heart was kind.

It may be presumed that the glint of sun striking on the silver castle was the first gleam of the rising sun. If it was, Lord Peter's party for the King lasted all night. Presumably the Troll had been hiding in some caves during the hours of daylight. It is a well-known characteristic of the Trolls that they cannot endure the light of the sun. They either turn into stone or burst if a direct ray of sunshine falls on them.[3]

The motif of disenchantment by decapitation is used by Mme d'Aulnoy in 'The White Cat'. As in many of Mme d'Aulnoy's fairytales, the motifs of this tale belong to the traditional folktales, and the general theme of the plot is traditional too. It is the tale of three sons sent out by their father on quests, in this case to determine the succession to the throne – a common motif. In this as in most tales of this type the youngest is the hero, and succeeds, while his elder brothers fail. The type has world-wide distribution, and the enchanted maiden is in the form of a toad, a mouse, a cat, etc.

Mme d'Aulnoy's amplification contains a good many details that are not characteristic of a folktale, but she succeeds in making the little white cat into an endearing character. As she tells it the tale is a long one, but, though it is shortened here, it will be found pleasant reading in its entirety.

Once upon a time there was a king who had three brave and handsome sons. As they grew to be men he began to be afraid that one or other of them would covet his throne, and it struck him that it would be wise to employ them in a series of quests. He summoned them to his presence and spoke very lovingly to them, saying that he thought the time was coming when he should resign the throne to one of them, but that they all had such good qualities that he could not decide between them, and he had made up his mind to send them on a quest, and the winner of it should be crowned King.

'When I have abdicated,' he said, 'I shall retire to a country place and give up all active employments. I shall need a quiet, gentle companion, so I want you to find me a little dog, not a great hound, but the smallest and gentlest and most beautiful dog you can find. I will furnish you with ample means, and you must ride out separately, and return in a year's time.'

The three princes were very much surprised to find their father in such a mood, but they had been thinking him rather old for some time, and were glad to have some prospect of getting into the saddle, so they provided themselves with all that they needed and rode to a castle a league from the city where they feasted together and promised that they would always remain friends and that whichever of them won in the contest would share his goods with the others. They agreed to meet in the castle on that day next year, and parted lovingly. All three had adventures, but we will only follow the fortunes of the youngest.

He went alone and on foot, as the others did, and whenever he saw a small and beautiful dog he bought it, but if he saw a more beautiful one he bought it, and gave the dog he already had to the vendor, for he had no kennel-man with him to look after hundreds of dogs. He travelled on and on until he found himself lost in a deep forest. His latest little dog ran off hunting, and disappeared in the darkness, and a heavy storm came on. The youngest prince kept as straight a path as he could, and at length he saw a dim light before him, and made his way towards it eagerly. Guided by the light he came up to a most magnificent castle. The gate was of gold lit by carbuncles and the walls were of translucent porcelain, decorated with pictures illustrating all the famous fairy stories. He could have wandered round looking at them forever, but the storm lashed on him so heavily that he returned to the gate and pulled the golden chain which rang the bell. Immediately the gate was opened, but he saw no people, only a dozen pairs of hands, holding flambeaux. Brave as he was, the prince started back, but a sweet song of welcome rang out and the hands beckoned him in. He went forward, and the hands drew him on through a coral door into a saloon of mother-of-pearl and through a procession of chambers, each more magnificently furnished than the last. At length they stopped in a comfortable room, where he was set in an easy chair in front of a bright fire, his wet clothes were taken off, he was washed, combed, perfumed and dressed in exquisite clothes, in which he looked extremely handsome, and finally led into a beautiful dining hall, decorated with pictures of all the famous cats of history. A cloth was laid upon the table and there were two covers, each set with its own golden cutlery. Until this time he had only seen the hands, but now a group of cats came in carrying musical instruments, who went up to a small orchestra where they began to play and sing, or rather catterwaul, making the most extraordinary noises, so that the prince could not help laughing.

In a moment, however, a door opened and a procession came in. First there were two male cats in deep mourning and next there came a little figure covered with a heavy black veil, followed by a number of other cats, some of them carrying cages filled with rats and mice.

The little figure came forward and put her veil back and the prince saw the most beautiful little white cat that ever was or ever could be. She looked very youthful and very sad, and she began to speak to him with such a sweet and soft mewing that it went straight to his heart.

'Son of a king,' she said to the prince, 'You are welcome. My mewing majesty beholds you with pleasure.'

'Madam cat,' replied the prince, 'It is very generous of you to receive me with such attention, but it is plain that you are no ordinary cat. Your gift of speech and the magnificence of your castle are proof enough of that.'

'I pray you, pay me no compliments,' she said. 'I am plain in my speech and manners, but I wish you well. Come, let them serve supper,' she continued, 'and bid the concert cease, for I see the prince does not understand what they are singing.'

The supper was served up, soup of mice for the cat princess and of pigeons for the prince. The White Cat considerately informed him that they were cooked in separate kitchens, and he ate with a good appetite. As they were talking he noticed a miniature hanging from a bracelet round her little wrist, and asked to see it, for he was interested in such things. He thought it would be a portrait of some prince of the cats, but to his surprise it was the picture of a young man of great beauty and strikingly like himself. He gave it back to her in silence, and she received it with an air of so much sadness that he said no more about it, but changed the talk to topics of the day, in which she showed herself well informed. After supper they went to watch a ballet performed by twelve cats and twelve monkeys – a very spirited performance. When it was over the White Cat wished him good night, and the attentive hands led him to a most elegant bedroom where they undressed him for bed.

Next morning the prince was roused early for a great hunt, in which the White Cat took part, having cast aside her mourning veil for the time being. She was mounted on a monkey and the prince on a wooden horse which carried him with a swift and easy action. It was a magnificent hunt and they returned to a banquet, at the end of which the prince was served with a liqueur. At the first taste of it all memory of his father's quest and even of his native country faded from his mind, and he passed his days in perfect happiness at the court of the White Cat, growing more and more fond of its gentle little mistress. But she had not forgotten, and one day she said to him; 'Son of a King, do you know that it is now three days to the time when you must meet your brothers, and that they have with them several beautiful little dogs.'

The whole memory raced back into the prince's mind and he was filled with dismay.

'Good Heavens!' he cried. 'What have I been about to forget everything. Where can I find a dog in the time? And where shall I find a horse that will carry me all those leagues to my father's Palace?'

The White Cat said to him, with great sweetness, 'Son of a King, do not distress yourself. I am your friend. You may yet stay one day here. It is five hundred leagues to your father's Court, but the good wooden horse will carry you there in twelve hours.'

'Beautiful cat,' said the prince, 'How can I thank you enough. But I must not only return to my father, I must bring him a little dog.'

'Take this acorn,' said the White Cat. 'Inside it is a little dog as beautiful as the dog-star.'

'Dear madam cat,' said the prince, 'surely you are jesting with me.'

'Put your ear to the acorn and listen,' replied the White Cat, and when the prince lifted the acorn to his ear he heard a tiny 'bow-wow.' The prince was delighted, but the White Cat told him to keep the little dog warm and safe in the acorn and not open it except in the King's presence.

They spent a happy day together, and next morning the prince mounted the wooden horse, and it carried him like the wind, so that he arrived at the castle where he was to meet his brothers the day before they did. This gave him time to consider what he should say about his little acorn-dog which he was to show first of all to the King, and he found he did not want to talk to his brothers about the little white cat whom he loved so dearly, so he went down to the castle kitchen and borrowed a turn-spit dog to pass off as his choice. It was a poor enough specimen, but he had no time to look about him. Before he could even clean it up his brothers arrived and saw the wooden horse curvetting gently in the courtyard.

The princes drove together in a coach. The two elder ones had each several baskets of delicate and beautiful little dogs to show to the king, and the turn-spit made himself very disagreeable by scratching all the way. The two elder princes exchanged glances, and each thought he was rid of at least one rival.

The King received them most affectionately and the elder boys showed off their pets and the King praised them all, but said they were all so beautiful that he could not tell which to choose. The two brothers began to dispute for the right of succession when the youngest took the acorn out of his pocket and opened it very carefully. The tiniest dog in the world was lying inside on a piece of cotton. It got up, wagged its tail, and began to dance a saraband. It was the most beautiful little creature that ever was seen, and there was no doubt at all which took the prize. But the King did not mean to give up his crown so easily.

'My dear boys,' he said, 'This little dog is certainly the smallest, and perhaps even the most beautiful but I fear he will be too delicate to live. I will keep all three dogs with me, and in the meantime, I will send you out on another quest. I will give you a year to bring me a length of cloth so fine that it will go through the eye of a needle used to make Valenciennes point-lace. I doubt if more than one of you will be successful in that.'

The two elder brothers were ready to agree to that, for it gave them another chance, but the youngest brother was angry. However he said nothing and went back with his brothers to the castle, where he returned the turn-spit to the kitchen, and parted with his brothers. It was less cordial than the first parting, for the two elders could not quite forgive the trick he had played them with the turnspit. The youngest prince mounted his wooden horse and rode away like the wind. He had no doubt where he wanted to go.

The horse carried him so swiftly that it was the night of the same day when he arrived at the castle, but all the doors were open and lights were shining from the walls. The hands were waiting for him. Some helped him to dismount and led the wooden horse into the stable, the rest led him to the White Cat's room. She was lying on a satin cushion in her little basket covered with her black veil; but when he came into the room, she sprung out of bed and came frolicking towards him. 'Oh you are come!' she said. 'Fate has used me so ill until now that I hardly dared to expect to see you again. Now we can be happy. But you have come without the crown that you have earned. How is that?'

The prince told her of how his father had put them off with another quest, and one that would be difficult to fulfil.

'But let my Father keep his kingdom,' he said. 'I had rather be here with you than reign in the finest kingdom in the world.'

'I know your good heart, and I trust it,' said the White Cat, 'but it is right that you should gain what you have earned. We have some skilled weavers among our Court, and I myself will put a claw into this. I will consider the matter, and in the meantime we have a year to enjoy ourselves.'

And indeed it was a year of happiness, and the prince became more and more full of admiration for all the talents and powers of that little gentle White Cat. He would have lost count of the months and days but the cat kept watch for him, and to impress the King that he was not to be set aside she sent him to Court in a splendid equipage, magnificently escorted, and gave him a walnut which, she said, contained such a cloth that the King could not reject it. The passage of the chariot was swift, but it was a little slower than the wooden horse, and when the prince arrived at the King's Court his brothers were already there, showing off their webs of cloth, which were indeed marvellously fine, so that they would go through the eye of a coarse pack-thread needle. But the King insisted on the needle which he had provided, which was meant to receive only the finest thread. The discussion was waxing hot when the prince's magnificent cavalcade arrived. It made some stir, but the prince came quietly into the room and saluted his father respectfully. 'Perhaps we shall find what we want inside this nut,' he said.

He cracked it, and there was a hazel nut inside. He cracked that, and inside it was a cherry stone. He cracked that, and inside it was its kernel; he cut the kernel carefully in two, and inside it was a grain of wheat. The King began to smile, and the brothers to nudge each other. He opened the wheat and inside was a grain of millet. Then the prince's heart began to fail, and he muttered under his breath, 'Oh my White Cat, have you betrayed me?' At that he felt a sharp scratch on his hand, and a drop of blood started out.

He opened the millet seed very carefully and drew out a most beautiful cloth, four hundred ells in length, wonderfully wrought with natural objects and the portraits of all the reigning monarchs of the world, but so fine that it would pass through the minute eye that the King presented to it. There was no doubt at all that the prince was the winner, but the King still clung to his crown. He besought his sons to gratify him by one more test of their obedience. It was necessary that a King should be married. Let the princes go out into the world again and each bring back with him a beautiful woman to be his bride. And he who brought back the most beautiful should be the King, and on the same day he should marry his wife. The King vowed that there should be no further delay.

All the injustice of this broke on the prince. He had won the award twice over and his successes were made to count as nothing. He said no word, but bowed and went back to his chariot.

This time the White Cat was awaiting him and she knew what had been decreed by the King. He was received triumphantly, for she believed that the time of her happiness was at last approaching. The year sped by happily until the day before which they must be ready to depart. But when the White Cat told the prince what he must do to procure her happiness he was filled with horror. He must cut off her head and her tail and throw them into the fire. 'I! Blanchette! My love! I be so barbarous as to kill you! Ah, you would doubtless try my heart; but indeed it is incapable of such ingratitude.'

At length by earnest entreaties she persuaded him that she believed it to be the beginning of their happiness, and with trembling hand he drew his sword and cut off her head and tail. No sooner had he thrown them in the fire then the little body grew and changed into that of a young maiden, who rose up so beautiful, noble and gentle that he could only stand and gaze at her in incredulous delight. Whilst he was still silent with rapture the doors opened and a number of lords and ladies came into the room with catskins over their shoulders and gathered round their queen to kiss her hands. They were followed by those humbler members of her court who had been invisible except for their hands. Queen Blanchette greeted each of them with joy and kindness, and then asked them to leave her with the prince, to whom she related her story.

She had been the daughter of a king, but her mother, in the course of her travels, had come to a fairy orchard and had been seized with an insane longing to taste its fruits. This was so ungovernable that it brought her to the point of death, and at length the fairies allowed her to devour as much fruit as she would on the condition that she gave her daughter to them as soon as she was born. The King tried in vain to keep his little daughter, but was at length forced to let her go. The baby was sedulously taught and watched over by the fairies but brought up in solitude with a parrot and little dog as her only companions. At length she saw and spoke with a beautiful and noble king who was hunting in the hills nearby. The princess's tower was guarded by a dragon and the two lovers were in great danger.

To complicate matters the fairies decided to marry the princess to a particularly hideous dwarf, and on the night when the lovers had planned to escape the dwarf arrived in his fairy chariot, burst in at the princess's window and called the dragon to destroy the king. The angry fairies turned the princess and all her subjects into

cats and put her into one of her father's castles. By this time her
father and mother were dead and she was the rightful queen of six
countries. But she could not be disenchanted from the spell that
hung over her except by a man exactly like her murdered lover.
Good fortune had sent the prince to her castle, and now she could
begin to be happy again.

The next day the pair set out for the prince's kingdom. The
other princes had brought beautiful brides with them, but when
Blanchette's beauty burst on the King he involuntarily exclaimed,
'Behold the incomparable beauty who deserves the crown!' This
admission was all that the young queen required. She refused to
deprive the King of his kingdom for she had six of her own
already. Instead she proposed to give the King one of her own,
and one to each of the brothers. Three kingdoms would be
enough for her and her husband, all she asked was the King's
friendship and his consent to her marriage with his son. It will be
imagined that this was readily conceded; the three weddings were
celebrated immediately, and after several months of celebration
the monarchs settled into their respective kingdoms.[4]

This tale is in the regular tradition of folk fairytales, and is, as I
have said, very widely distributed. A more unusual Scandinavian
story with the motif of an enchanted human who is finally
disenchanted, but not by decapitation, is to be found in Andrew
Lang's *The Brown Fairy Book*. It is taken, he says, from *Neuis-
ländischen Volksmärchen*, but he described it as 'Adapted', which
means no doubt that it has been somewhat altered. I have been
unable to trace the original, but the tale is worth giving, even in its
altered form.

Kisa the Cat

Once upon a time there lived a queen who had a beautiful
cat, the colour of smoke, with china-blue eyes, which she
was very fond of. The cat was constantly with her, and ran
after her wherever she went, and even sat up proudly by her
side when she drove out in her fine glass coach.

'Oh, pussy,' said the queen one day, 'you are happier than
I am! For you have a dear little kitten just like yourself, and I
have nobody to play with but you.'

'Don't cry,' answered the cat, laying her paw on her

mistress's arm. 'Crying never does any good. I will see what can be done.'

The cat was as good as her word. As soon as she returned from her drive she trotted off to the forest to consult a fairy who dwelt there, and very soon after the queen had a little girl, who seemed made out of snow and sunbeams. The queen was delighted, and soon the baby began to take notice of the kitten as she jumped about the room, and would not go to sleep at all unless the kitten lay curled up beside her.

Two or three months went by, and though the baby was still a baby, the kitten was fast becoming a cat, and one evening when, as usual, the nurse came to look for her, to put her in the baby's cot, she was nowhere to be found. What a hunt there was for that kitten, to be sure! The servants, each anxious to find her, as the queen was certain to reward the lucky man, searched in the most impossible places. Boxes were opened that would hardly have held the kitten's paw; books were taken from bookshelves, lest the kitten should have got behind them, drawers were pulled out, for perhaps the kitten might have got shut in. But it was all no use. The kitten had plainly run away, and nobody could tell if it would ever choose to come back.

Years passed away, and one day, when the princess was playing ball in the garden, she happened to throw her ball farther than usual, and it fell into a clump of rose-bushes. The princess of course ran after it at once, and she was stooping down to feel if it was hidden in the long grass, when she heard a voice calling her; 'Ingibjörg! Ingibjörg!' it said, 'have your forgotten me? I am Kisa, your sister!'

'But I never had a sister,' answered Ingibjörg, very much puzzled; for she knew nothing of what had taken place so long ago.

'Don't you remember how I always slept in your cot beside you, and how you cried till I came? But girls have no memories at all! Why, I could find my way straight up to that cot this moment, if I was once inside the palace.'

'Why did you go away then?' asked the princess. But before Kisa could answer, Ingibjörg's attendants arrived breathless on the scene, and were so horrified at the sight of a strange cat, that Kisa plunged into the bushes and went back to the forest.

The princess was very much vexed with her ladies-in-waiting for frightening away her old playfellow, and told the queen who came to her room every evening to bid her good-night.

'Yes, it is quite true what Kisa said,' answered the queen; 'I should have liked to see her again. Perhaps, some day, she will return, and then you must bring her to me.'

Next morning it was very hot, and the princess declared that she must go and play in the forest, where it was always cool, under the big shady trees. As usual, her attendants let her do anything she pleased, and, sitting down on a mossy bank where a little stream tinkled by, soon fell sound asleep. The princess saw with delight that they would pay no heed to her, and wandered on and on, expecting every moment to see some fairies dancing round a ring, or some little brown elves peeping at her from behind a tree. But, alas! she met none of these; instead, a horrible giant came out of his cave and ordered her to follow him. The princess felt much afraid, as he was so big and ugly, and began to be sorry that she had not stayed within reach of help; but as there was no use in disobeying the giant, she walked meekly behind.

They went a long way, and Ingibjörg grew very tired, and at length began to cry.

'I don't like girls who make horrid noises,' said the giant, turning round. 'But if you want to cry, I will give you something to cry for.' And drawing an axe from his belt, he cut off both her feet, which he picked up and put in his pocket. Then he went away.

Poor Ingibjörg lay on the grass in terrible pain, and wondering if she should stay there till she died, as no one would know where to look for her. How long it was since she had set out in the morning she could not tell – it seemed years to her, of course; but the sun was still high in the heavens when she heard the sound of wheels, and then, with a great effort, for her throat was parched with fright and pain, she gave a shout.

'I am coming!' was the answer; and in another moment a

cart made its way through the trees, driven by Kisa, who used her tail as a whip to urge the horse to go faster. Directly Kisa saw Ingibjörg lying there, she jumped quickly down, and lifting the girl carefully in her two front paws, laid her upon some soft hay, and drove back to her own little hut.

In the corner of the room was a pile of cushions, and these Kisa arranged as a bed. Ingibjörg, who by this time was nearly fainting from all she had gone through, drank greedily some milk, and then sank back on the cushions while Kisa fetched some dried herbs from a cupboard, soaked them in warm water and tied them on the bleeding legs. The pain vanished at once, and Ingibjörg looked up and smiled at Kisa.

'You will go to sleep now,' said the cat, 'and you will not mind if I leave you for a little while. I will lock the door, and no one can hurt you.' But before she had finished the princess was asleep. Then Kisa got into the cart, which was standing at the door, and catching up the reins, drove straight to the giant's cave.

Leaving her cart behind some trees, Kisa crept gently up to the open door, and, crouching down, listened to what the giant was telling his wife, who was at supper with him.

'The first day that I can spare I shall just go back and kill' he said; 'it would never do for people in the forest to know that a mere girl can defy me!' And he and his wife were so busy calling Ingibjörg all sorts of names for her bad be-haviour, that they never noticed Kisa stealing into a dark corner, and upsetting a whole bag of salt into the great pot before the fire.

'Dear me, how thirsty I am!' cried the giant by-and-by.

'So am I,' answered his wife. 'I do wish I had not taken that last spoonful of broth; I am sure something was wrong with it.'

'If I don't get some water I shall die,' went on the giant. And rushing out of the cave, followed by his wife, he ran down the path which led to the river.

Then Kisa entered the hut, and lost no time in searching every hole till she came upon some grass, under which Ingibjörg's feet were hidden, and putting them in her cart, drove back again to her own hut.

Ingibjörg was thankful to see her, for she had lain, too frightened to sleep, trembling at every noise.

'Oh, it is you' she cried joyfully, as Kisa turned the key. And the cat came in, holding up the two neat little feet in their silver slippers.

'In two minutes they shall be as tight as ever they were!' said Kisa. And taking some strings of the magic grass which the giant had carelessly heaped on them, she bound the feet on to the legs above.

'Of course you won't be able to walk for some time; you must not expect that,' she continued. 'But if you are very good, perhaps, in about a week, I may carry you home again.'

And so she did; and when the cat drove the cart up to the palace gate, lashing the horse furiously with her tail, and the king and queen saw their lost daughter sitting beside her, they declared that no reward could be too great for the person who had brought her out of the giant's hands.

'We will talk about that by-and-by,' said the cat, as she made her best bow, and turned her horse's head.

The princess was very unhappy when Kisa left her without even bidding her farewell. She would neither eat nor drink, nor take any notice of all the beautiful dresses her parents bought for her.

'She will die, unless we can make her laugh,' one whispered to the other. 'Is there anything in the world that we have left untried?'

'Nothing except marriage,' answered the king. And he invited all the handsomest young men he could think of to the palace, and bade the princess choose a husband from among them.

It took her some time to decide which she admired the most, but at last she fixed upon a young prince, whose eyes were like the pools in the forest, and his hair of bright gold. The king and the queen were greatly pleased, as the young man was the son of a neighbouring king, and they gave orders that a splendid feast should be got ready.

When the marriage was over, Kisa suddenly stood before them, and Ingibjörg rushed forward and clasped her in her arms.

'I have come to claim my reward,' said the cat. 'Let me sleep for this night at the foot of your bed.'

'Is that all?' asked Ingibjörg, much disappointed.

'It is enough,' answered the cat. And when the morning dawned, it was no cat that lay upon the bed, but a beautiful princess.

'My mother and I were both enchanted by a spiteful fairy', said she, 'and we could not free ourselves till we had done some kindly deed that had never been wrought before. My mother died without ever finding a chance of doing anything new, but I took advantage of the evil act of the giant to make you as whole as ever.'

Then they were all more delighted than before, and the princess lived in the court until she, too, married, and went away to govern one of her own.[5]

9

Benevolent Cats in Fairy Tales

We have heard much in the last two chapters of the sinister ways of cats and of wicked old witches masquerading in cat shape, but there are quite a number of stories of benevolent and kindly cats, although these belong more to fairytales than legends, and the kindly and protective cats are quite often human beings transformed by magic into animal forms. We are not actually told in Peter Buchan's story 'The Black Cat' that the old woman who advised the hero was a fairy, but it seems likely. The story is a mere summary of the plot, but it has some interesting points.

Tom, the hero, the only son of an old Fifeshire farmer, was a lazy lie-about, who had no fancy for any work, so he enlisted as a soldier. He soon found he had no taste for that either. He had taken the bounty and squandered it away, and his Colonel, who was a harsh man, shipped him overseas where the Governor treated him very ill, so that he determined to desert. He fled to a distant part of the country, for he knew that he would be shot if he was caught, and since he had no friends and no money he was in a bad way. But he fell in with an old woman who treated him so kindly that he trusted her with his secret and asked her advice. She suggested that he should lay his case before the King and ask for redress. He did as she suggested and the King set him a task – to go to a neighbouring castle and spend the night there. On his way he called in on the old woman who told him that he must speak to a black cat which would appear to him and ask it to advise him.

He made his way into the castle, and waited hours there, pensive and uneasy. At about midnight a black cat came in.

'Come away, my bonny cat!' he said gladly. 'I have been long awaiting you.'

'Who bade you speak?' she said. He told her about the old woman. She said, 'There will be three men come in, but never do anything they request of you, till one of higher deportment arrives, and when I touch you, do as he bids you.'

With that the cat sat down by him, and in a little time three men came in, who said to him fiercely: 'Rise, and let us sit down.' But he stayed where he was and said nothing. Then another man came in, and said, 'Follow me,' and he felt the Black Cat touch him, so he rose and followed the man into another room. Here he stopped and spoke. 'I was once the King of this castle, but was murdered by my Steward, who fled and covered his traces, and has since become Governor of the Island on which you were stationed. Tell this to my son who is now King, so that the false Steward may be punished. The three men that you saw were hired to do the murder. When the wrong is avenged we shall all depart and the castle will be no longer haunted.' With that he disappeared.

Tom went to the King, who gave him a letter to the Commander-in-Chief. Tom got safely back to his regiment, where he met one of his old comrades, who was very sorry for him, for his coming had been reported to the Colonel, and his friend feared for his life.

'You can save me,' said Tom, 'by taking this letter from the King direct to the Commander-in-Chief. But I beg you not to delay.'

His friend took it and at that moment a guard arrived to take him before the Colonel. He was court-martialled, and for all he could plead, was condemned to be shot. But before the sentence could be carried out, the Commander-in-Chief had read the letter, arrested the Governor and freed Tom to serve as witness. The Governor was taken before the King, and his guilt being proved, was immediately executed. Tom was made Governor in his place, and, since he was now in power, he reduced the Colonel to the rank of a private, promoted the friend who had helped him to the rank of officer, sent for his old father and lived happily with him ever after.[1]

This is a rather crude example of a widespread folktale – the disenchanting of a haunted castle – but the part that the cat plays in it is rather unusual. Occasionally the castle is haunted by cats.

A very pleasant story of a company of kind and grateful cats is a variant of the story of Kind and Unkind, without the motif of marriage with a prince. It is from Thorpe's *Yule-Tide Stories* and is to be found re-told in Andrew Lang's *Orange-Fairy Book*.

The Two Caskets

There was once an ugly, cross woman who had two daughters living with her, one her own daughter and the other her step-child. The daughter was as cross and ugly as her mother, and spoilt and petted besides, but the stepdaughter was kind, gentle and considerate, and very pretty too, so that she had a good word from everyone and all the neighbours loved her. This love and esteem in which she was held made the other two dislike her more and more, so that their hatred became a frenzy and they determined to get rid of her. So one day the stepmother called the two girls to bring their spinning wheels out to the well and to sit on the edge and spin there. 'And be careful what you do,' she said, 'for the first one that lets her thread break, down into the well she goes.' But she did not play fair, for her own daughter got the finest flax to spin, but the other was given mere refuse, all tangled and lumpy and weak, so, careful though she was, her thread was bound to snap soon, and when it did the stepmother rushed out of the house, picked up her legs and shot her down into the well. 'Good riddance to bad rubbish!' said the wicked pair, and went laughing into the house. But the good stepdaughter fell and fell, until at the bottom a door seemed to open in the ground, and she fell softly through on to a grassy bed of flowers, with the frightened tears still wet on her cheeks. She found herself in a fair land, with trees and grass and flowers, and the birds singing all about, though there was no sun above her, and a light like early morning. There seemed no way out of the land, and she was afraid of her stepmother's cruelty, so she got up and went to seek her fortune. There was a narrow path leading through the trees and she followed it until it came into the open through a field and she came to a rickety fence, all overgrown with old-man's beard. As she looked along it to find a low place to cross the fence spoke to her. 'Dear little maiden; please do me no harm. I'm am an old fence, so old and decayed.' 'Don't be afraid, dear fence,' said the girl, 'Indeed I will do you no harm.' She climbed over the fence, very lightly and carefully, so that not a plank moved, and went on her way. And the silver fronds of the old-man's beard waved after her and the fence murmured after her; 'All good luck go after you, my considerate child!' The next thing that the girl noticed was an oven that stood close by the path, full of warm, new-baked bread, with a peel lying by it, and she paused, for she was very hungry, and the oven spoke to her. 'Dear little maiden, please do me no harm. I am only a poor oven! Take out and eat as much as you want, but take nothing with you and put back what you do not eat.' 'Indeed I would not hurt you, kind oven,' said the girl. She opened the oven door and drew out one loaf on the peel and sat down to eat it. She only needed half, so she put what was left back in the oven and put the peel where she had found it, thanked the oven kindly for its hospitality and went on her way. And the oven wished her good fortune in the world.

After a while the girl came to a meadow where a cow was grazing, with a pail hung on its horn. Her udder was so full that it was plain she needed milking. The cow looked round to her and said: 'My dear, good lass, do me no harm. I am only a poor cow. Drink as much of my milk as you want but do not scatter my milk on the ground. Pour what is left over my hoofs, and hang the pail on my horn.' 'Indeed, dear cow, I would not harm you,' said the girl. 'It is very kind of you to let me drink your milk.' She milked the cow gently and deftly into the pail, took a long drink of the milk, and emptied what was left very carefully over the cow's hoofs. Then she stroked the cow and thanked it and went on her way. And the cow mooed after her, 'Good luck go with you, my gentle lass.'

The next thing the girl saw was a very old apple tree, whose boughs almost touched the ground, laden with fruit, some green and some red and juicy. And the tree called out to her: 'My dear little girl, please do me no harm; I am so old and bent. Gather as many of my ripe fruits as you need, but carry none away with you. Eat what you need and bury the rest at my root. But prop my bending branches before you go.' The girl did exactly as he said, propped the bending branches carefully, and went on her way. And the tree called after her; 'May all good go with you, my considerate maiden.'

After this the road grew wider, and the girl saw a very old woman with long white hair leaning on a gate. The girl came up to her, and said: 'Good evening, dear mother!'

The old woman said: 'And good evening to you again. Who are you, who greets me so kindly?' 'I am only a poor stepchild,' said the girl, 'and I am seeking service in this world which is strange to me.' 'If that's so,' said the old woman, 'You can spare time to wait a little and comb my hair for me. And we can talk while you do it.' 'Indeed I will,' said the girl, and she combed it most carefully. When she had finished the old woman said: 'Since you didn't think yourself too good to comb me I will tell you where you can find a service. Be discreet and all will go well with you.' She then directed the girl where to go, and gave her much good advice as well. The girl listened most carefully, thanked her and went by the way she had directed. There she found a large farm where they were in need of a serving maid to milk and tend the cows and to sift the corn in the barn. So she was engaged for a year. She was to start on her duties in the morning. That night she had her supper and went to bed.

Early in the morning, as soon as it was light, the young girl started on her work. She went into the cow house and made friends, patting and stroking them and speaking to them gently. Before she milked them she fetched hay and straw, and fed them, swept out the cow house and made all neat and comfortable. Then she fetched the pails and stool and sat down to milk them. They in their turn were as gentle and loving as she was. Each one lowed with pleasure when she came up, and played no tricks on her; not one of them kicked the pail over or lashed about with its tail, but they all stood as quiet as lambs, and let down their milk willingly.

Indeed it was a pleasure to see how the little girl set about her duties and how well she and the cows got on together. When the milking was done the girl carried the pails into the dairy next door and strained the milk and collected it into the measure, and as she was doing this a great company of cats came in, a multitude of them, great and small, mewing round her so earnestly that her soft heart was touched, saying:

'Give us a little milk!
Give us a little milk!'

The girl looked round and saw a great shallow bowl on the floor, evidently meant for the cats.

'My poor little pusses' she said. 'I daresay you are all very hungry and thirsty. Wait, I will give you something to drink.' With that she lifted one of the pails and filled the big flat bowl. The cats all took their turn, and as they finished they gathered round the girl, rubbed themselves against her knees, arched their backs and purred with delight, so that it was a pleasure to see how they caressed the little serving maid.

When she had finished her work in the cow-byre the girl went into the big barn to sift the corn, and she worked long and hard, riddling and sifting, till she had made a great pile of the good grain and the chaff was all swept into one corner. As she was still at work a great flight of sparrows came down into the yard and hopped nearer and nearer to the barn, picking what they could from the ground and fluttering

131

nearer to the great barn. At length they hopped on to the high threshold of the door, and began chirping all together:

'Give us a little corn!
Give us a little corn!'

'My poor little sparrows!' said the girl. 'You have a hard life, I am sure, picking up what little bits you can find. Wait, I'll give you something to eat.' And she picked up a few handfuls from the heap, and scattered the grain amongst them, and sparrows came fluttering about her, pecking and fluttering their wings, and were so glad, just as if they would thank the little girl for being so kind to them.

So the time passed, day after day, and every day the little maid cared for the cows and fed and groomed and milked them, so that they grew sleek and plump, and there never was a greater abundance of milk or finer cattle on the farm either before or since. And every day she gave the cats their share of milk and every day the sparrows were given their handfuls of corn and all the farm was happy and prospered.

One day the mistress of the farm sent for the little step-daughter and said to her: 'I have noticed how well you keep the cows and how willingly you do all that you are set to do. Now I want to see what you make of more difficult work. Take that sieve, carry it to the stream and bring it back full to the brim without spilling a single drop.'

The girl did not see how she could do that, but it was her business to obey her mistress, so she picked up the sieve and went down to the stream. And a flight of sparrows followed her. The little maid dipped the sieve carefully in the water and lifted it gently up, but the water ran so quickly through every hole that it was all gone by the time the sieve reached shoulder level, and at last, wet and cold, she burst into tears. Suddenly there was a twittering from the boughs that sur-rounded the pool, where all the sparrows had gradually gathered together. The girl though they were trying to cheer her, so she dried her eyes to listen to their chirping. But it was words they were singing:

'Ashes in sieve,
Then it will hold!

> Ashes in sieve,
> Then it will hold!'

they sang again and again. She thought perhaps they were right, so she jumped up and ran and fetched ashes, and packed the bottom of the sieve carefully with them and when she lowered it gently into shallow water the ashes swelled, and held the water without a drop leaking as she carried it home.

The old woman was amazed, and said: 'I never knew you had so much knowledge. Who instructed you in this?' But the girl said nothing, for she was afraid of getting the sparrows into trouble.

Time went on, and one day her mistress called the little stepdaughter again and said: 'Here are two skeins of wool, but the black skein is not black enough and the white is not white enough, so take them down to the stream and wash them till the white skein is black and the black skein is white.'

There seemed no sense in this to the girl, but she was used to trying to obey her stepmother's commands, however unreasonable, so she took the two skeins down to the stream, and some of the sparrows went after her. The poor girl washed and scrubbed, but the white skein remained white and the black, black, until at last at the thought of disappointing the mistress who had spoken so kindly to her, she burst into tears; but at this there was a great twittering of the sparrows, and when she lifted her head to listen she heard them singing in human words:

'Take the black,
Turn to the east!
Take the black,
Turn to the east.'

She knew they were trying to help her, so she picked up the black skein and waded upstream to the east, until she came to a pool in which she could dip it. She had only dipped it and lifted it out when it turned a dazzling white, and she was going to try washing the white skein when the birds cried out again:

'Turn to the west!
Turn to the west!
Take the white
And turn to the west!"

So she waded down the stream, and stood looking westward, and after one dip the skein turned a deep rich black; the sparrows flew twittering away, and the girl carried them down joyfully to her mistress, who was absolutely amazed, and asked her again who had helped her, but the girl only smiled and said nothing, for she would not betray the kind little sparrows.

After that all went smoothly, until her mistress called the little stepdaughter before her again, and said: 'There is one last task for you to do, and then there will be no more. Here are the two skeins that you washed. You must weave them up before the sunset hour, and they must be smooth and even, with no breaks or joins, and when that is done I shall be satisfied.'

The girl took the skeins and went to the room where the loom was kept. But when she began to set up the skein her heart sank, for it was like the flax her stepmother had given her. It was all in short pieces, lumpy and uneven. Even to set up a smooth warp was impossible, and when it came to the weft, it was still worse. And this was her last test! She leant forward on her stool and cried bitterly. All at once the door was pushed open and the long procession of cats came into the room. They rubbed themselves against her, purring loudly, and asked her what was the matter. She told them all about it, and showed them the lumpy thread and broken ends. They sat down and purred loudly. Then the leader cried: 'Leave this to us, we can easily finish before the sunset hour. You have always been kind and loving to us, and now we have the chance to repay you.' With that all the cats jumped up to the loom. They pulled out the lumps or lengthened the short threads, and licked and twisted the broken ends, so that they joined like magic. Then the cats jumped on to the loom and clattered it to and fro, so that in no time at all the yarn was woven, and it was close and fine and even, better than any human hand could do it. The girl ran down with it gladly to her mistress, who was amazed at the workmanship. 'I never knew you could do a piece of work like this!' she said. 'Who taught you such a craft?' But the girl smiled gently and said nothing, for she did not want to betray her dear friends the cats.

After that all went well until the year came to its end, and then the girl began to feel that she must go into the upper world again, though everyone was kind to her in the under-world, and she hated to leave her friends the cats, and the little sparrows and her dear cows. But a longing was on her to see the sun again and to feel the free air of the upper world. So she went to her mistrss and asked to be released from her service. Her mistress said, 'I am sorry to lose you, but I cannot keep you if you wish to go. You have pleased me in everything, so I should like to give you a reward for your services. Go up to the attic above this room and you will find a number of caskets. Choose any one you like and you may take it home; but do not unlock it until you put it into the place where you mean to remain.' The girl thanked her mistress, and climbed up into the attic, and the cats streamed up after her. The attic was filled with caskets, of all sizes, shapes and colours, so that it took quite a time to look at them all. Some of them seemed to the girl too grand to be payment for her work when she had had good food and lodgings, and kindness too from men and beasts. And as she was puzzling over them the cats all called out 'Take the black! Take the black!' She looked all round, and in a far corner she found a little, strong black casket with a key hanging from its handle. So she said, 'Yes, of course, dear pussies, that's the one for me.' And she took it down to show to her mistress, who said: 'You have made a wise choice. Goodbye, my girl, good fortune will go with you.' The girl thanked her mistress with great gratitude for her beautiful present, and for all her kindness and said goodbye to her; and then she said goodbye to her cats and her sparrows and her cows, and that was a sad farewell indeed, for they could hardly bear to lose her, and indeed everyone on the farm was sorry when she went. Her journey back was quicker going than coming, and when she got to the place where the well had been a door opened in front of her and she went up a steep staircase which came out into the upper world just by the well. So she went into her old home, where her stepmother and stepsister were surprised and angry to see her. 'Well,' said her stepmother, 'I thought you were dead long ago, and your bare bones lying at the bottom of the well. Life is full of disappointments! Where have you been all this long time?' 'I went down into the underworld', said the stepdaughter, 'and took service for a year. And, look, they gave me this good black box for my wages. May I have a corner where I can keep it?' 'What insolence!' said her stepmother. 'As if we'd clutter our nice house with you or your dirty black box either. Be off with you!' Then she thought that the neighbours might talk; for they had been rather disagreeable about the disappearance of the girl. So she added – 'If you must stay be off into the henhouse, and set up your dirty box there.' So the girl went off, and she swept and washed and cleaned the henhouse, and found a nice corner where she could keep her box. Then she unfastened the key from the handle and unlocked it. Such a light burst out as she lifted the lid that she started back. Shining gold and diamonds and rubies and emeralds flashed out of it, so that the old rickety henhouse looked as if it was on fire and all the neighbours round rushed in to the rescue. They saw the jewels before the two wicked ones did, and it was perhaps just as well for the girl, for all the neighbourhood came to look until they all knew every jewel in the box, and the stepmother dare not take so much as a brooch or a ring, for it would be recognised. And those two were ill with envy, so that they could not sleep nor eat. They knew most of what had happened to the girl from the talk of the neighbours, and at last they determined that the stepsister would do better, for they were both sure that she was worth twenty of the poor little stepdaughter. So one fine day the stepmother made her daughter sit on the well-curb and thrust her down into the cold deep well. She wasn't sure at the last that she really wanted to go, but when she landed on the bed she was quite reassured and sure that she would make her way and bring back something far handsomer than her sister's box. So she got up and went on her way, but she was disgusted by the rickety old fence that she came across first, and affronted that it had the impertinence to speak to her. She tore up the palings and pulled off the old man's beard, and went on quite triumphant, never hearing that the paling called after her; 'You shan't have done this to me for nothing.' As she started, so she went on. She tore off the oven door, scattered the loaves and broke the peel. When she had drunken all the milk she wanted she threw what was left over the ground, and broke the pail. She shook all the apples over the ground and broke down the branches. And after her came again and again the muttered curse, 'You shan't have done this to me for nothing.' It can be imagined how furious she was at being asked to comb the old woman's hair. She thrust past her through the gate, slamming it behind her so fiercely that she nearly knocked the poor old woman down, and the curse that went after her this time concluded 'Continue in the same wickedness and you will see how it will go with you in the world.'

In spite of this, however, she was engaged as a maid-servant, for they had been without one since her step-sister left them, and she was as cruel and bad as the little maid had been good. The poor cows were half starved, ill-kept and roughly used. They were thin and wretched, and had little milk to give. Sometimes too they kicked over their pails which made matters worse. As for the cats, when they appeared begging for milk, she hit them, threw things at them and drove them away. She threw stones at the sparrows and chivvied them into the wood, so that there was no more merry chirping about the farmyard. But indeed there was not much grain to spare, for the cats dare not come into the barns to keep down the rats and mice. In fact the whole farm suffered from her cruel ways. All the same the mistress kept her on and in course of time set her the same tests as she had set to her stepsister. But there were no sparrows or cats to help her so she failed dismally. When her time came to give her notice the mistress took it willingly and told her that she was the worst maid she had ever had. All the same she allowed her to choose a casket in payment for her year's service. The girl hurried up to the loft and chose the largest and gaudiest casket she could see. She said goodbye to no one, but hurried home with it and was eagerly greeted by her mother who admired the casket as well as she did. They took it up to the best bedroom and eagerly unlocked it, expecting to be dazzled with light cast by the jewels. A light did dazzle them indeed, but it was of a real flame, leaping up, which licked round the walls and set the roof on fire. The neighbours rushed out, but the house burnt like tinder and the wicked mother and daughter were consumed with it. Only the little henhouse, standing apart, was safe from the flames, and there the stepchild lived a happy peaceful life, beloved by all her neighbours and kind to all living things. And when she died the box was the heritage of all considerate girls, and by its help they can always keep themselves neat however little they have. And so the story ends.[2]

A story on very much the same theme is to be found in *The Crimson Fairy Book*. The source is probably Sicilian, since Andrew Lang mentions Sicilian tales in his preface, and 'Father Gatto' is the name of the Chief Cat. I have not, however, managed to trace the story. It is about a colony of cats inhabiting a large house by themselves.

In the days when animals could talk there was a large house not far from a populous town and almost entirely inhabited by a tribe of cats. Cats were much respected in that country because in the past they had freed it from a terrible plague of rats and mice. They made a happy community except that they liked to have their housework done for them, and, as they were rather exacting masters they found it difficult to keep their human servants. Girls only went into their service if they could get no other and therefore on the whole they were not much good at their work.

It happened that in the neighbouring town there lived a widow woman with two daughters. The elder was lazy and selfish, and not even very pretty but the mother loved her far better than Lizina the younger girl who had to do all the work, often with no better reward than a beating. One day she felt that she could bear it no longer, and she exclaimed, 'If you hate me so much you will be better without me. I am going to live with the cats!' 'Be off with you then!' said her mother, and seized an old broomstick from behind the door. Poor Lizina knew better than to linger; she sped out of the house, and half an hour later she was knocking at the door of the Cat's Colony.

They were glad to welcome her, for that very day a member of the household had fallen out with the cook, who had run out at the end of the dispute with the marks of ten claws on her face.

Lizina found it a strange place to work in at first. The cats could talk, but they purred and mewed more than they talked, and at first she found it hard to understand them. She began to cook the dinner, but she felt it would be easier to do it without quite so much supervision. There were cats everywhere – cats under her feet and on the draining board and on the table as she was cleaning the vegetables, and peeping into the oven when she opened it and walking about the shelves among the pots and pans, purring loudly all the time. This was a sign of their approval, but she did not quite understand at first. However, she was a sweet-tempered, kind girl and she was used to working under difficulties. She was concerned about the little kittens who were under everybody's feet. She found a cozy place for them, and picked them up and settled them, stroking them so that they gave their little purrs, and after she had washed up the dinner she coaxed the oldest cat, who was lame, on to her knee and stroked her until she went happily

139

asleep. They were all delighted with her. As time went on and she learned the ways of the house she did better and better. She kept the house beautifully, with sparkling windows and shining pots and the floors clean enough to eat your meals off them. She plumped up the pillows and nursed the cats who were sick or hurt, she played with the kittens and took care to give the cats just what they liked to eat. They all doted on her.

After a time they had a visit from the old father cat, Father Gatto, who lived all alone in a barn higher up the hill. He was very taken with Lizina the moment he saw her. 'Are you well served by this nice, black-eyed little person?' he said to the colony, and they all replied with one voice; 'O yes, Father Gatto! We have never had so good a servant.' And every time he came they gave the same answer, purring and rubbing themselves against her.

Lizina loved the cats and was happy with them, but as time went on she began to long for her own kind and grew homesick for her mother and her sister Peppina, harshly though they had treated her, and old Gatto, who had become very fond of her, noticed that she often looked sad, and that sometimes she had been crying, and at last he asked her what was the matter. 'Have any of my children been unkind to you?' he said. 'Oh no, they are all kind and loving,' she said, 'but I do so long to get back to my mother and sister.' Old Gatto was sad at this, but he would not keep her against her will and he said she must be rewarded for all her kindness to his children, so he led her down the cellar stairs and unlocked the door of a great vaulted room under the house. There were two big earthen jars standing there, one was full of oil, the other of golden liquid so bright that it sent out a light. 'I will dip you into one of these jars,' he said, 'which will you choose?' Lizina peeped into both of them, but she thought the gold jar was too grand for her, so she said 'Please dear Father Gatto, dip me into the oil.' 'No, no, you are too good for that,' said Father Gatto, 'the golden jar for a golden girl.' And he picked her up and dipped her into the golden jar. As he lifted her out the whole cellar was lit up. Her hair was still black and there was a rosy glow on her cheeks, but all the rest of her, clothes and all, shone, so that she looked like a moving statue of pale gold.

'You will find your wages in your pocket when you get home,' said Father Gatto, 'and I have this piece of advice for you: when the cock crows turn your head and look at him, but turn your back on the ass if he begins to bray. Good luck go with you.' Lizina kissed Father Gatto's white paw and thanked him for his great kindness, said goodbye to all the cats who grieved bitterly at losing her, and set out for home. As she reached her mother's door the cock crowed out loud. She remembered what Father Gatto has said and turned to look at him, and immediately a star shone out on her forehead. A moment later the donkey brayed in the field nearby, but she kept her back to it, and went into the house. Her mother and her sister Peppina hardly knew her at first until she spoke to them, but when she took her handkerchief out of her pocket and a dozen pieces of gold fell out of it they greeted her joyfully, and picked up the pieces. Peppina wanted above everything to wear Lizina's golden clothes, but they would only shine on Lizina, so she and her mother had to content themselves with the golden coins that she found in her pocket every day.

At first everything went well, and Lizina was happier at home than she had ever been, but reports of her beauty spread all over the country and presently a young Prince came to visit her and fell deeply in love with her, and she with him. At this Peppina's jealousy flared up and she could not even pretend to be kind to her sister, and when it came to talk of marriage she determined to go to the Cat Colony and come back a golden girl like her sister. So very early one morning she set out and was soon knocking at the door of Cat Castle. In the meantime the cats had missed Lizina so much that they could not bring themselves to engage another servant; but when Peppina told them that she was Lizina's sister they engaged her at once. The little kittens said to one another, 'She is not like our Lizina,' but the old grave cats rebuked them, and said, 'You cannot expect all servants to be pretty. She has been brought up in the same house and trained in the same neat ways.' They soon found that the kittens were right. In the first place Peppina would allow no one in the kitchen. She hustled them all out and locked the door, and when one dashing young cat jumped in at the window she hit him so hard with the rolling pin that she cracked his ribs. She used her leisure in sitting by the fire and eating tit-bits. The meals were scrambled together anyhow, the beds were hardly made, and dust lay in all the corners. Besides this her temper was so bad that no cat, young or old, was safe. Father Gatto heard sad stories when he came down to inspect the new maid.

'You've been here long enough,' he said to her. 'Come down to the cellar and get the wages you have earned.' Down they went and he asked her which of the two jars she deserved to be dipped into. 'Into the gold one of course,' she said. 'You're a liar!' said Father Gatto. 'It's the other you've earned.' And he flung her in, heels over head. When she scrambled out, oil from head to foot, Father Gatto knocked her on to the ash-heap, and rolled her over until she was filthy and half blinded, and as she staggered off he called after her. 'If you want your wages be careful to turn towards the ass when it brays!' Peppina, howling and sobbing, made her way home as best she could. As she got to her mother's gate the ass brayed loudly and she turned towards it, hoping for pockets full of gold. Then she gave a louder yell than ever, for she felt something thrusting out of her forehead, and putting up her hand she felt a donkey's tail. Then she yelled twice as loud and ran into the house, where it took Lizina three hours, buckets of hot water and all the soap they had in the house to get her clean. But nothing would remove the donkey's tail. Just as they had given it up a messenger arrived in the house to say that the Prince would come with a carriage to fetch his bride next day. As soon as the messenger had gone the widow seized the broomstick, beat Lizina with all the strength of her arm, pushed her down into the well-house and locked her in.

When the Prince called for his bride next day a maiden was waiting for him wrapped in a thick white veil. It was Peppina, with her donkey's tail coiled round under her head-dress. The Prince handed her into the carriage and rode off beside her. On his way into the city he passed Cat Castle, and the cats were at every window for they had heard that the Prince was marrying the most beautiful girl in the country with a star in the middle of her forehead, so they knew it must be their dear Lizina and they were all agog to see her pass. But when the coach came up a great wawling arose from every one of them, and all together they sang:

'Mew Mew: Mew Mew!
Prince choose your bride anew

For hid at home is fair Lizina;
All you've got is foul Peppina.'

The coachman drew rein. 'The cats say you've not got the right bride, your Highness. They say take another look.'

The Prince leant into the coach and turned back the bride's veil.

'They're right!' he said. 'Turn back,' and the coachman drove back like the wind. The Prince leapt off his horse and drew his sword. In a moment he was in the house, and had seized the cruel mother. 'You wicked woman!' he said. 'Take me to the true bride or feel my sword!'

With his sword still at her back she unlocked the well-house, and the star on Lizina's forehead shone out of the darkness like the sun. The servants had thrown Peppina out of the coach and the Prince handed Lizina into it with joy. As they passed Cat's Castle all the cats came out with Father Gatto at their head, and followed them into the cathedral, where Lizina and the Prince were married amidst great rejoicing.[3]

These cats were true cats, it seemed, but they had some magic powers, almost as if they had been fairies.

A cat who was an entirely unmagical character, and yet played a part in the hero's good fortune is that best known to us in England in the legend of 'Dick Whittington and his Cat'. This is an international tale which has somehow become attached by the slenderest of threads to Sir Richard Whittington, the well-known Lord Mayor of London in the reign of Henry V. The legend as it is told has nothing to do with the biography of Richard Whittington, who was the son of a well-to-do family among the Gloucestershire squires, who were well able to afford the apprenticeship of their son. In fact, the tale of a cat who makes her master's fortune because he can sell her in a cat-less country over-run with rats and mice is so widely found as to be almost world-wide. The Stith-Thompson Type Index lists twenty-six countries where it is found. One of the most engaging and unusual is the Icelandic version, 'The Cottager and his Cat' retold in Andrew Lang's *Crimson Fairy Book*.

There was once a royal city which stood very near to a great forest which was scantily inhabited. In the forest there was a wretched little hut inhabited by an old man and woman who had one young son. They lived as if they were very poor but in fact the old man had a great deal of money hidden away, but he was a miser who starved himself, his wife and his son so that he could amass money to hide away about the house. In the end he starved himself to death and his son began to find secret hoards of gold in all kinds of nooks and crannies. As he went to bed that night he was thinking that at last he and his mother would be able to live in comfort after years of starvation. Thinking this he fell asleep.

In his sleep a strange man appeared to him and said:

'The money that you will find about your father's hut is all
ill-gotten, and was squeezed out of the poor. Do not use it.
Half of it you must return to the poor and the other half you
must throw into the sea. Watch, however, after you have
flung it, and if anything floats to the surface, even a piece of
paper, fish it out, it is yours by right.'

The young man woke from the dream and lay for the rest of the night more and more disturbed, for it seemed to him a true vision. He told his mother and she wept and said she feared it was only too true that his father had been cruel to the poor, so he searched all about and found a quantity of money and he and his mother divided it into two parts, and he took one half and went into the village and gave it to all the poorest people, particularly to those who had been ruined by his father. Then he took the other half and went to the sea-side, scrambled out to a big rock where the water was deep and threw it all into the sea. It sank down and down out of sight, but the waves tossed up one little screw of paper, and when he picked it up six shillings were inside it. It was a small enough sum with which to start in the world, but it was better than nothing, so he put it in his pocket and went home. For the next few weeks he worked hard in the garden, and there were enough vegetables to keep him and his mother, and their consciences were at rest. But one morning he got up and found that his mother had died in her sleep. All the villagers came and helped at her funeral; but when they had buried her he felt very sad and lonely, and he wandered off into the forest to make a living for himself.

He walked and walked and walked until he was quite lost, and he saw a cottage with a light coming from it, and knocked at the door. An old woman opened it, and he asked her if he might have a drink of milk. She spoke kindly and invited him in, saying that they could put him up for the night. There were three men at supper and two women, and they invited him to sit down with them, and gave him a good supper. When he had finished he began to look round. There was a good fire in the hearth, and in front of it sat a little animal such as he had never seen before. It was grey, and it had bright green eyes and was making a strange little singing sound such as he had never heard in his life. When he stroked it it rubbed itself against him. 'What do you call this beautiful little animal?' he said. 'We call it a cat,' said the old woman. 'My brother brought it from across the sea.'

'I am all alone, and I should like it for company,' said the young man. 'How much would it cost to buy it?' The sailor brother said, 'I will let you have it for six shillings,' and the young man loved the cat so much that he exchanged it for all the money he had.

Next morning he set out with the cat wrapped in his cloak. He walked through the forest all day until he reached open country and he knocked at the door of a cottage. A man came to the door and the young man said: 'My cat and I are very hungry, but I am afraid we have no money to pay for food.' 'Then we shall have to give it to you for nothing,' said the man, and led him in to the house where there were two women. They were charmed with the pretty little cat, and gave it all kinds of things to eat, and it rubbed itself against them and purred and patted them gently with its paws. They were so kind that he told them all his story and asked their advice.

The man said 'We are not far from the town here. Go to the King's palace and ask for an audience. The King is kind and wise, and he will advise you what to do.'

In the morning the young man went to the palace and asked for an audience. After a time he was admitted into the Great Hall where the King was dining. No sooner were the dishes set down than swarms of dark creatures came out from every hole and corner, climbing on to the table and eating from every dish. One came on to the King's plate, and when the King struck at it it bit him.

'What are those horrid creatures?' said the young man.

'They are rats,' said the King. 'They swarm over the city and infest the palace, and we have tried every means against them in vain.'

As he spoke the young man felt his cat struggling out of his arms. In a flash he was on the table, and in three seconds six rats were lying dead. In a few seconds dozens more were lying dead and the whole army of rats were flying in a panic.

'What is that wonderful creature?' said the King.

'It is called a cat' said the young man 'and yesterday I bought it with all the money I had.'

'Stay with us,' said the King, 'and clear the city of this plague. And for the luck you have brought us I will give you this choice: Be my Prime Minister or marry my daughter and rule the kingdom after me.'

'If you please, your Majesty,' said the young man, 'may I marry your daughter?'

And so it was.[4]

In spite of its fairytale ending this is hardly a real fairytale, for there is no magic in it, except the vision, and the cat has no supernatural qualities.

'Puss-in-Boots', best known in Perrault's version, is a true fairytale, with a talking cat and an ogre. It is too well known to be given here, and I have already given a version of it, 'Lord Peter', in Chapter Eight, for the sake of its enchanted lady.

10

Monsterous Cats

The traditional monster against which a knight shows his courage is a dragon or worm, and these as a rule belong to the genus *dragon* and are comparatively common. Dragons do not usually need to be accounted for; they are natural hazards. (Occasionally, however, one appears as a consequence of impious behaviour, like the Lambton Worm, which was fished out of the River Wear by the wild young Heir of Lambton, who was fishing on a Sunday when all good people were going to church.) Giants and monstrous wild boars are also taken for granted, though these are occasionally domesticated and set on by witches. Monstrous cats are much less common, and are generally accounted for by some human impiety or breach of taboo. One of the early exploits of King Arthur is to be found in the thirteenth-century prose romance of *Merlin*, generally called *The Vulgate Merlin*.[1] Lady Wilde, while on the subject of cats, gives a lively version of this story founded on a Cambridge manuscript edited by Mr Wheatley. Here we have the cat, pretty clearly a form of the Devil, which is fished out of the sea by a fisherman who grudges the gift of a fish which he had promised to God.

Merlin told the King that the people beyond the Lake of Lausanne greatly desired his help, 'for there repaireth a devil that destroyeth the country. It is a cat so great and ugly that it is horrible to look on.' For one time a fisher came to the lake with his nets, and he promised to give Our Lord the first fish he took. It was a fish worth thirty shillings; and when he saw it so fair and great, he said to himself softly, 'God shall not have this; but I will surely give him the next.' Now the next was still better, and he said, 'Our Lord may wait yet awhile; but the third shall be His without doubt.' So he cast his net, but drew out only a little kitten, as black as any coal.

And when the fisher saw it he said he had need of it at home for rats and mice; and he nourished it and kept it in his house, till it strangled him and his wife and children. Then the cat fled to a high mountain, and destroyed and slew all that came in his way, and was great and terrible to behold.

When the King heard this he made ready and rode to the Lake of Lausanne, and found the country desolate and void of people, for neither man nor woman would inhabit the place for fear of the cat.

And the King was lodged a mile from the mountain, with Sir Gawain and Merlin and others. And they clomb the mountain, Merlin leading the way. And when they were come up, Merlin said to the king, 'Sir, in that rock liveth the cat'; and he showed him a great cave, large and deep, in the mountain.

'And how shall the cat come out?' said the King.

'That shall ye see hastily,' quoth Merlin; 'but look you be ready to defend, for anon he will assail you.'

'Then draw ye all back,' said the King, 'for I will prove his power.'

And when they withdrew, Merlin whistled loud, and the cat leaped out of the cave thinking it was some wild beast, for he was hungry and fasting; and he ran boldly to the King, who was ready with his spear, and thought to smite him through the body. But the fiend seized the spear in his mouth and broke it in twain.

Then the King drew his sword, holding his shield also before him. And as the cat leaped at his throat, he struck him so fiercely that the creature fell to the ground; but soon was up again, and ran at the King so hard that his claws gripped through the hauberk to the flesh, and the red blood followed the claws.

Now the King was nigh falling to earth; but when he saw the red blood he was wonder-wrath, and with his sword in his right hand and his shield at his breast, he ran at the cat vigorously, who sat licking his claws, all wet with blood. But when he saw the King coming towards him, he leapt up to seize him by the throat, as before, and stuck his fore-feet so firmly in the shield that they stayed there; and the king smote him on the legs, so that he cut them off to the knees, and the cat fell to the ground.

Then the King ran at him with his sword, but the cat stood on his hind-legs and grinned with his teeth, and coveted the throat of the King, and the King tried to smite him on the head; but the cat strained his hinder feet and leaped at the King's breast, and fixed his teeth in the flesh, so that the blood streamed down from breast and shoulder.

Then the King struck him fiercely on the body, and the cat fell head downwards, but the feet stayed fixed in the hauberk. And the King smote them assunder, on which the cat fell to the ground, where she howled and brayed so loudly that it was heard through all the host, and she began to creep towards the cave; but the King stood between her and the cave, and when she tried to catch him with her teeth, he struck her dead.

Then Merlin and the others ran to him and asked how it was with him.

'Well, blessed be our Lord!' said the King, 'for I have slain this devil, but, verily, I never had such doubt of myself, not even when I slew the giant on the mountain; therefore I thank the Lord.'

'Sir,' said the barons, 'ye have great cause for thankfulness.'

Then they looked at the feet which were in the hauberk, and said, 'Such feet were never seen before!' And they took the shield and showed it to the host with great joy.

So the King let the shield be with the cat's feet; but the other feet he laid in a coffin to be kept. And the mountain was called from that day 'the Mountain of the Cat', and the name will never be changed while the world endureth.[2]

This monstrous cat had certainly an indomitable spirit. It will be noted, by the way, that its sex changes three-quarters of the way through the narrative. People always find it an effort to call a cat 'he'.

Ruth Tongue's story of the Four-Eyed Cat which was given in Chapter Five is also relevant here, as the Four-Eyed Cat is a genuine monster, but one to be propitiated; there is obviously no hope of destroying it since it has become an elemental creature, though in a more restricted area than Shony, or Davy Jones. Davy Jones generally claimed his tribute for himself, but Shony, a sea creature of the Isle of Lewis, was given a tribute of specially brewed ale at Hallowtide, for which a return of washed-up seaweed was expected in order to manure the fields.

The catastrophe of 'The Four-Eyed Cat' is caused not by impiety but by the infringement of a taboo, perhaps the best-known of all the fishermen's prohibitions, that which forbids the presence of a woman on board, or even the mention of a woman.[3]

In George Henderson's *Survivals of Beliefs Among the Celts* he cites a passage out of Fled Bricrend, an early Irish tale out of *The Cuchulainn Saga*, in which the hero and his companions are visited by three great magical cats.

One night as their portion was assigned the heroes, three cats from the cave of Cruachan were let loose to attack them, i.e.

three beasts of magic. Conall and Loigaire made for the rafters, having left their food with the beasts. In that wise they slept till the morrow. Cuchulainn fled not from his place from the beast which attacked him. But when it stretched its neck out for eating, Cuchulainn gave a blow with his sword on the beast's head, but the blade glided off as 'twere from stone. Then the cat set itself down. In the circumstances Cuchulainn neither ate nor slept. As soon as it was early morning the cats were gone.

Clearly these cats are representative of another-world power: and are thought of as one of the disguises under which the other-world magician tests the hero, one of a series of tests through which Curoi, such is the magician's name, awards the palm for bravery to Cuchulainn.[4]

It is likely, as George Henderson suggests, that these formidable cats were shape-shifters, since the Cave of Cruachan was similar to the Enchanted Cave of Cesh Corran, that home of magic and danger, in the Fionn legends.

The story of another formidable and dangerous cat is to be found in an excellent article in *The Ulster Tatler* by E. M. Griffith, 'The Heart of Down.' There is a touch of wry humour about it, for it is the story of The Man Who Killed the Wrong Cat. This creature was so infamous that several places were named after him. He lived at the Stone of the Great Cat in County Down, and devastated the country far and wide. At length the King of Uladh (Antrim and Down) offered a large reward and the hand of his daughter in marriage to any man who would destroy the beast. The challenge was taken up by a chieftain called O'Rooney. He rode up to Cloughmaghrecat, routed the cat out of its lair, and chased it past Ballymahinch and Saintfield. Just past Saintfield at Drumreagh, he overtook it, and there the print of his horse's hoof is to be seen on one of the gravestones, as the hound Cabyll's footprint was left in token of Arthur's great hunting of the wild boar Trwyth in the Mabinogion. He cut off its head at Ballyking (the Town of the Head), dragged its body through the ford of Annaghcat (the Marsh of the Cat), disembowelled it at Drumbuig (the Hill of the Belly), and proudly claimed his reward, which was given with honourable promptitude. Alas, it was a gift pleasanter to give than to receive, for the Princess proved to be a terrible shrew, and she made poor O'Rooney so miserable that, to his dying day, he was heard to murmur 'I killed the Wrong Cat'.[5]

11
Nursery Tales and Amusements

The two fireside animals, the dog and the cat, are naturally the two creatures which catch the child's eyes first, and after them are the cocks and hens, the birds that come picking up crumbs on the windowsill, and, in the country kitchen, the little mouse that pops in and out of holes by the fireplace.

The hereditary enmity between cat and mouse is a standing subject. A mouse's frustration is rather pleasingly expressed in a rhyme in Chamber's *Popular Rhymes of Scotland*.

> There was a wee bit mousikie
>   That lived in Gilberaty, O,
> It couldna get a bite of cheese
>   For cheetie-poussie-cattie, O.
> It said unto the cheesikie:
>   'O fain wad I be at ye O,
> If 'twere na for the cruel paws
>   O' cheetie-poussie-cattie, O'[1]

(Scots rhymes and stories are generally more rhythmic than the English ones, though rather more difficult to understand.)

The English 'Mouse and Mouser' is a plain dialogue which illustrates the sinister character of the cat, from the mouse's point of view.

The Mouse went to visit the Cat, and found her sitting behind the hall door, spinning.

Mouse: What are you doing, my lady, my lady?

Cat: I'm spinning old breeches, good body, good body.

Mouse: Long may you wear them, my lady, my lady.
Long may you wear them, my lady.

Cat: I'll wear 'em and tear 'em, good body, good body.
I'll wear 'em and tear 'em, good body.

Mouse: I was sweeping my room, my lady, my lady.
I was sweeping my room, my lady.

Cat: The cleaner you'd be, good body, good body.
The cleaner you'd be, good body.

Mouse: I found a silver sixpence, my lady, my lady.
I found a silver sixpence, my lady.

Cat: The richer you were, good body, good body.
The richer you were, good body.

Mouse: I went to the market, my lady, my lady.
I went to the market, my lady.

Cat: The further you went, good body, good body.
The further you went, good body.

Mouse: I bought me a pudding, my lady, my lady.
I bought me a pudding, my lady.

Cat: The more meat you had, good body, good body.
The more meat you had, good body.

Mouse: I put it in the window to cool, my lady, my lady.
I put it in the window to cool, my lady.

Cat: The faster you'd eat it, good body, good body.
The faster you'd eat it, good body.

Mouse: The cat came and ate it, my lady, my lady.
The cat came and ate it, my lady.

Cat: And I'll eat you, good body, good body.
And I'll eat you, good body.[2]

The Scottish version has both rhyme and rhythm, but has a good many words in it which are unfamiliar to southern ears – the *kiln-ring*, for instance, the place in a barn where the grain is dried, *weel may he brook it*, may he appreciate it, like it, *soopit*, swept, *coft*, bought, *kitchenless*, without food *loesome*, lovesome, and so on.

> The Cattie sits in the kiln-ring,
>   Spinning, spinning;
> And by came a little wee mousie
>   Rinning, rinning.
>
> 'O what's that you're spinning, my loesome,
>   Loesome lady?'
> 'I'm spinning a sark to my young son,'
>   Said she, said she.
>
> 'Weel mot he brook it, my loesome,
>   Loesome lady.'
> 'Gif he dinna brook it weel, he may brook it ill,'
>   Said she, said she.
>
> 'I soopit my house, my loesome,
>   Loesome lady.'
> ''Twas a sign ye didna sit amang dirt then,'
>   Said she, said she.
>
> 'I fand twall pennies, my winsome,
>   Winsome lady,'
> ''Twas a sign ye warna sillerless,'
>   Said she, said she.
>
> 'I gaed to the market, my loesome,
>   Loesome lady.'
> ''Twas a sign ye didna sit at hame then,'
>   Said she, said she.
>
> 'I coft a sheepie's head, my winsome,
>   Winsome lady.'

''Twas a sign ye warna kitchenless,'
    Said she, said she.

'I put it in my pottie to boil, my loesome,
    Loesome lady.'
''Twas a sign ye didna eat it raw,' ,
    Said she, said she.

'I put it in my winnock to cool, my winsome,
    Winsome lady.'
''Twas a sign ye didna burn your chafts then,'
    Said she, said she.

'By came a cattie, and ate it a' up, my loesome,
    Loesome lady.'
'And sae will I you – worrie, worrie – guash, guash,'
    Said she, said she.[3]

Chambers quotes the enthusiastic account of the narrator from
whom he learned the poem.

The gentleman who communicated the above added the
following note: 'This is a tale to which I have often listened
with intense interest. The old nurse's *acting* of the story was
excellent. The transition of voice from the poor obsequious
mouse to the surly cat, carried a moral with it; and when the
drama was finished by the cat devouring the mouse, the old

nurse's imitation of *guash*, *guash* (which she played off upon the youngest urchin lying on her lap) was electric! Our childish pity for the poor mouse, our detestation of the cruel cat, and our admiration of our nurse, broke out in, with some, crying – with some, "curses not loud but deep" – and, with others, kisses and caresses lavished on the narrator.'[4]

In a good many nursery tales the cat presents the final solution, as, for example, in 'The Old Woman and the Pig'.

An old woman was sweeping her house, and she found a little crooked sixpence. 'What,' said she, 'shall I do with this little sixpence? I will go to market and buy a little pig.' As she was coming home she came to a stile; but the pig would not go over the stile. She went a little further and she met a dog. She said to the dog:

> 'Dog, dog, bite pig!
> Pig won't get over the stile;
> And I shan't get home tonight.'

But the dog would not.

The old woman went on in growing frustration, every agent that she tried to enlist to help her refusing, until at last she met a cat. So she said:

> 'Cat, cat, kill rat!
> Rat won't gnaw rope;
> Rope won't hang butcher;
> Butcher won't kill ox;
> Ox won't drink water;
> Water won't quench fire;
> Fire won't burn stick;
> Stick won't beat dog;
> Dog won't bite pig;
> Pig won't get over the stile;
> And I shan't get home tonight!'

The cat said, 'If you will give me a saucer of milk, I will kill the rat.'

So the old woman gave the cat the milk, and when she had lapped up the milk,

> The cat began to kill the rat;
> The rat began to gnaw the rope;
> The rope began to hang the butcher;
> The butcher began to kill the ox;
> The ox began to drink the water;
> The water began to quench the fire;
> The fire began to burn the stick;
> The stick began to beat the dog;
> The dog began to bite the pig;
> The pig in a fright jumped over the stile;
> And the old woman got home that night.[5]

In some versions the cat began voluntarily to kill the rat, but in most they cannot refrain from showing the cat's policy of enlightened self-interest.

In many rhymes and stories the cat comes in to give a tragic ending to a festive occasion, as in 'Puddock, Mousie', which is an earlier form of 'The Frog's Wooing' than the nineteenth–century music hall version which conquered the nursery.

> *The Puddie and the mouse*
> There lived a Puddy in a well,
>   Cuddy alone, cuddy alone;
> There lived a Puddy in a well,
>   Cuddy alone and I.
> There was a Puddy in a well,
> And a mousie in a mill;

Kickmaleerie, cowden down,
Cuddy alone and I.

Puddy he'd a-wooin' ride,
Sword and pistol by his side.

Puddy came to the mouse's wonne:
'Mistress Mouse, are you within?'

'Yes, kind sir, I am within;
Saftly do I sit and spin.'

'Madam, I am come to woo;
Marriage must I have of you.'

'Marriage I will grant you nane,
Till Uncle Rottan he comes hame.'

Uncle Rottan's now come hame,
Fye, gar busk the bride alang.

Lord Rottan sat at the head o' the table,
Because he was baith stout and able.

Wha is't that sits next the wa',
But Lady Mouse, baith jimp and sma'?

Wha is't that sits next the bride,
But the sola Puddy wi' his yellow side?

Syne came the Deuk but and the Drake,
The Deuk took the Puddy, and gart him squaik.

Then came in the carle Cat,
Wi' a fiddle on his back:
'Want ye ony music here?'

The Puddy he swam down the brook,
The Drake he catched him in his fluke.

The Cat he pu'd Lord Rottan down,
The kittlins they did claw his crown.

But Lady Mouse, baith jimp and sma',
Crept into a hole beneath the wa';
'Squeak!' quo' she, 'I'm weel awa'.'[6]

It is interesting to see how often the cat is introduced as a musician, from

> Hey diddle, diddle,
> The cat and the fiddle[7]

onwards. Whether there is some connection with catgut is a matter for conjecture. A fiddle seems to come first to mind, but a cat is also supposed to perform on the bagpipes.

> A cat came fiddling out of a barn,
> With a pair of bag-pipes under her arm;
> She could sing nothing but fiddle cum-fee
> The mouse has married the bumble-bee.
> Pipe cat; dance mouse
> We'll have a wedding at our good house.[8]

Iona and Peter Opie quote a similar rhyme from Crane's *Baby's Bouquet*

> Pussy-cat high, Pussy-cat low,
> Pussy-cat was a fine teazer of tow.
> Pussy-cat she came into the barn,
> With her bag-pipes under her arm.
> And then she told a tale to me,
> How Mousey had married a bumble-bee.
> Then was I ever so glad,
> That Mousey had married so clever a lad.[9]

Here the cat musician is a benevolent character.

In both England and Scotland there are a number of short little rhymes for dancing children up and down.

> Pussicat, wussicat, with a white foot,
> When is your wedding and I'll come to it.
> The beer's to brew the bread's to bake.
> Pussycat, pussycat, don't be too late.[10]

or

> Poussikie, poussikie, wow!
> Where'll we get banes to chow?
>   We'll up the bog,
>   And worry a hogg,
> And then we'll get banes enow.[11]

There are various rhymes which imitate animal noises, often building up by repetition, like that which begins:

> I had a wee cock and I loved it well,
> I fed my cock on yonder Hill,
>   My cock, lily cock, lily cock, coo;
> Everyone loves their cock, why should not I love my cock too?

It builds up by repetition, until in the end we have:

> I had a wee pig and I loved it well,
> I fed my pig on yonder hill;
> My pig, squeakie, squeakie.
> My cat, cheetie, cheetie,
> My dog, bouffie, bouffie,
> My sheep, maie, maie,
> My duck, wheetie, wheetie,
> My hen, chuckie, chuckie,
> My cock, lily-cock, lily-cock, coo;
> Everyone loves their cock, why should not I love my cock too?[12]

A similar English song begins:

> I had a cat, and the cat pleased me,
> And I fed my cat under yonder tree,
> And the cat went fiddle-i-fee. [13]

One short Scots rhyme given in Chambers is an imitation of the cat's purring.

> Dirdum drum
> Three threads and a thrum,
> Thrum gray, thrum gray. [14]

If the rs are rolled after the Scots fashion it makes a sound very like a cat's purring.

There are one or two laments for a cat's death, such as:

> The craws hae killed the poussie, O,
> The craws hae killed the poussie, O;
> The mickle cat sat down and grat
> In Jeanie's wee bit housie, O. [15]

The Scots version of 'Ding, Dong, Dell', ends with an invitation to the funeral, so that in that version the rescue was too late, but in the English version we are allowed to hope, for it goes,

> Ding, dong, dell,
> Pussie's in the well!
> Who put her in?
> Little Tommy Green.
> Who pulled her out?
> Little Johnnie Stout.
> What a naughty boy was that
> To try to drown poor pussy-cat,
> Who never did him any harm,
> But kill'd the mice in his father's barn. [16]

Arthur Rackham at least takes it that the effort was unsuccessful, for the little dripping cat who is lifted out looks fully alive. One may take it that this rhyme is a piece of propaganda on behalf of ill-treated cats, as much as 'I love little Pussie' on the positive side of the question.

Of the folk games which deal with cats perhaps the best known is 'The Minister's Cat', a quiet fireside game, in which all the adjectives beginning with A are attached to The Minister's Cat until the ingenuity of the circle is exhausted when the company passes on to B. This is a forfeit game. 'The Priest Cat' is another fireside game, given in MacTaggart's *Gallovidian Encyclopedia*. It consists in passing a lighted stick from hand to hand repeating the rhyme:

> About wi' that, about wi' that
> And keep alive the priest cat.'

The one in whose hand it dies out pays a forfeit. MacTaggart says: 'Anciently when the priest's cat departed this life, wailing began in the countryside, as it was thought it became some supernatural being – a witch, perhaps of hideous form – so to keep it alive was a great matter.'[17]

This quotation is of special interest because it describes not only a traditional game, but one founded on a folk belief.

A more active cat game was 'Cat and Dog', a game between three players, something like stool-ball. There are two holes into which the 'cat' – a piece of wood about four inches long and one in diameter – is aimed, each of which is protected by a player holding a stick, called a 'dog'. If the cat gets into a hole, the thrower takes the stick and the protector takes the cat; if it is hit by the dog that counts as a run.[18]

'Tip Cat' or 'Cat and Kitten' is a game played by four or more players, with a short stick pointed at each end, called the cat or kitten, and a longer stick, which is the bat. The players stand at intervals round a ring and the striker is in the centre. Particulars of the rules are to be found in Lady Gomme's *Dictionary of British Folk-Lore, Part I, Traditional Games*.[19]

Another old and well-known game is 'Cat's Cradle', an entirely sedentary game played by two players with a piece of string as its sole apparatus.[20]

12
cats
in modern literary
folklore

The literary treatment of folklore themes in the sixteenth and seventeenth centuries was founded more directly upon folk tradition than upon scholarship, for many of the writers of that period came up from the country to make their fortunes in London, with a first-hand knowledge of the traditional country beliefs. These were, of course, sophisticated to please the taste of the town, but we can still deduce a good deal from them of the country beliefs and practices. Towards the end of the seventeenth century the antiquaries and learned men began to study the subject and to collect material. Aubrey's notes spring to mind at once, and there were other students of tradition, such as Glanvil, who make a significant contribution to our knowledge of folk beliefs. At the end of the eighteenth and the beginning of the nineteenth centuries the folklore collectors got to work, and many of them, such as Scott, Hogg and Henderson, had considerable first-hand knowledge, though their belief that the raw material of folklore needed embellishment to make it acceptable to the taste of the refined reader had an unfortunate effect on the literal accuracy of their reporting. By the end of the nineteenth century, however, we find a much nearer approach to scientific accuracy, and those fictional writers who wanted to use folk beliefs were well equipped with information. Until Dr Margaret Murray began to study the subject from a rather different angle there was no doubt in the mind of the average author that the belief in witchcraft was a pure superstition and that the supposed witches were the victims of malicious accusations or of pure delusion. We find that taken for granted in Charlotte Yonge's *Lances of Lynwood*[1] and in Scott's *Ivanhoe*.[2]

Dr Margaret Murray herself, indeed, was entirely sceptical about the actuality of witchcraft, but where she showed credulity was in failing to make allowance for the effect of torture and of suggestion on the witches under examination, and her tendency to trace the witchcraft practices to an ancient Stone Age fertility cult. It seems not unlikely that, in the general perturbation of Europe from the fifteenth to the seventeenth centuries, the rituals and practices described in the trials were actually practised by a minority of the population, and in our own disturbed times some young people find satisfaction in imitating them. The number of books written on the subject nowadays leaves people in no want of information about it.

In the nineteenth century J. H. Ewing wrote stories on fairy themes, including 'The Brownies', 'Lob-Lie-by-the-Fire', 'Amelia and the Dwarfs',[3] all showing a competent knowledge of folk traditions, but containing no reference to cats. Stories that touch on cats are most likely to deal with witchcraft; for, as we have seen in several of the previous chapters, cats have traditionally a close connection with witches, and it was not till the beginning of this century that witchcraft became a favourite subject for literary folklore.

One of the relatively early witchcraft stories to gain immediate popularity was John Masefield's *Midnight Folk*,[4] first published in 1927. This is a complicated story of the search for lost treasure by an evil coven of witches, led by their witch-master and of a small boy's attempts to foil them and to clear his great-grandfather's reputation from the slur cast upon it by a rumour that he himself was responsible for the disappearance of the treasure entrusted to him. In this the boy Kay Harker is helped by an honest cat and by a number of wild creatures, rather doubtful in some of their habits but of a fundamental honesty. There are three cats in the story, Blackmalkin and Greymalkin, both the witches' familiars, and Nibbins, who fundamentally disapproves of witchcraft but is strangely drawn towards the witchcraft practices. All three cats are members of Kay Harker's household, and the head of the coven is Kay's governess, whose magical pseudonym is Mrs Pouncer. Kay's further helpers are 'the guards' – the toys and playthings of which the boy had been deprived by his harsh governess. Nibbins first comes on the scene and takes charge when Kay had been sent early to bed and had gone to sleep.

After a time, he did not think that it was a guitar, but a voice calling to him: 'Kay, Kay, wake up.' Waking up, he rubbed his eyes: it was broad daylight; but no one was there. Some-one was scraping and calling inside the wainscot, just below where the pistols hung. There was something odd about the daylight; it was brighter than usual; all things looked more real than usual. 'Can't you open the door, Kay?' the voice asked. There never had been a door there; but now that Kay looked, there was a little door, all studded with knops of iron. Just as he got down to it, it opened towards him; there was Nibbins, the black cat.

'Come along, Kay,' Nibbins said, 'we can just do it while they're at the banquet; but don't make more noise than you must.'

Kay peeped through the door. It opened from a little narrow passage in the thickness of the wall.

'Where does it lead to?' he asked.

'Come and see,' Nibbins said.

Kay slipped on his slippers and followed Nibbins into the little passage; Nibbins closed the door behind him and bolted it.

'I'll lead the way,' he said. 'Mind the stairs: they're a bit worn; for the smugglers used to use these passages. But there's lots of light. Take my paw, as we go up.'

They went up some stairs in the thickness of the wall; then a panel slid up in front of them and they came out on to the top landing. Nibbins closed the panel behind them. It was dark night there on the landing, except for a little moon-light. The house was very still, but looking down over the banisters into the hall, Kay thought that he saw a shadow, wearing a ruff and a long sword, standing in the moonlight. The cuckoo-clock in the nursery struck twelve.

'All the house is sound asleep,' Nibbins said. 'Jane and Ellen are in there in those two rooms. They little know what goes on among us midnight folk. Give us a hand with this ringbolt, will you?'[5]

Through a trap-door which Kay had never seen before they went down a ladder into a little room hung with swords and banners which Nibbins called the guard-room. On the wall was a list of the guards, who had been Kay's old toys and imaginary playmates, but they had all gone away for a year because they had a clue to the treasure, and things had gone to wrack and ruin without them. Nibbins led Kay through the secret passage and Kay looked through the eyes of the portraits on the wall and saw into the drawing-room and dining-room.

What did he see?

There were seven old witches in tall black hats and long scarlet cloaks sitting round the table at a very good supper: the cold goose and chine which had been hot at middle-day dinner, and the plum cake which had been new for tea. They were very piggy in their eating (picking the bones with their fingers, etc.) and they had almost finished the Marsala. The old witch who sat at the head of the table tapped with her crooked-headed stick and removed her tall, pointed hat. She had a hooky nose and chin, and very bright eyes.

'Dear Pouncer is going to sing to us,' another witch said.
'Hear, hear,' the other witches said. 'Dear Pouncer, sing.'

'But you must join in the chorus, sisters. Shall it be the old song, Dear Nightshade?'

'Yes, yes; the old song.'

Mrs Pouncer cleared her throat and began:

> 'When the midnight strikes in the belfry dark
> And the white goose quakes at the fox's bark.
> We saddle the horse that is hayless, oatless,
> Hoofless and pranceless, kickless and coatless,
> We canter off for a midnight prowl . . .'

Chorus, dear sisters . . .

> 'Whoo-hoo-hoo-, says the hook-eared owl.'

All the witches put back their heads to sing the chorus:

> 'Whoo-hoo-hoo, says the hook-eared owl.'

It seemed to Kay that they were looking straight at him. Nibbin's eyes gleamed with joy.

'I can't resist this song,' he said, 'I never could. It was this song really, that got me into this way of life.'

'But I don't know what it means. What is the horse that is hayless?'

'Aha,' Nibbins said. 'Well, we've time while they're at this song: it has nine times nine verses; but you ought to stay for some more Whoo-hoos. Doesn't it give you the feel of the moon in the tree-tops?'[6]

In spite of the fascination of witch music Nibbins remains loyal to Kay, and he leads him up to the broomsticks' stable in one of the chimneys. They throw five broomsticks down to the ground and fly off on the remaining two, to escape from the witches and to watch a gathering of covens with their witch-master.

Blackmalkin and Greymalkin are wholly committed to witchcraft. They take their part in the magic ritual and Blackmalkin is ready to betray his old comrade, Nibbins, to the gamekeeper, which would have been his death if he had not discovered Blackmalkin's treachery. In the end the guards discover the treasure and the whole sinister gang are outwitted, so that all ends happily for little Kay Harker.

T. H. White's Arthurian tale, *The Sword in the Stone*,[7] has some resemblance in structure to this tale; but though there is a witch as well as a wizard, there is no cat, so that it does not touch upon our subject.

Nicholas Stuart Gray, an author of children's fairy stories and plays, who has a good supply of folklore materials, a keen sense of humour and a very alert interest in cats, has given us some magical variations on folk tales in which cats play an important part. Perhaps the most able of these is *The Stone Cage*,[8] first written as a puppet play, which is a variation of Grimm's *Rapunzel* told by the witch's two familiars, Tomlyn the cat and Marshall the raven. Tomlyn had been turned out of the woodcutter's cottage where he had lived as a kitten on a false accusation of having stolen food, which had actually been taken by the dog, and had been lured into a witch's hut, and lived long and wretchedly ever since. From this experience he had imbibed an aversion from human beings and a deep distrust of his own affections. He believed himself to be a tough and cynical character, but in spite of that he was fundamentally loving and very brave. The raven was a much softer character, but he was very timid, and assumed an air of learning to which he had no right.

Tomlyn sets out the situation clearly at the beginning:

Ever heard of 'a dog's life'? I'll bet you have. Everyone has. Means a low, miserable kind of life,. Full of kicks and curses, and nothing much to eat. I don't know, I'm sure – what about a cat's life, then? There's not much said about that, is there? *Nine* lives, yes – but what sort of lives are these supposed to be? I'll tell you the sort I had – a dog's life.

I have to admit it isn't every cat who lives with a witch, though.

And what a witch! Bad-tempered old – ! No, it's not fair to a cat or a she-dog, to liken her to one of them. Let's say she was a bad-tempered old belldam, and let it go at that. She hated people. She hated Marshall, her raven. She hated her bats and toads. She hated me. Sometimes I think she even hated herself. A great old hater, was madam.

And I was never all that besotted about her.[9]

The old witch set her trap to trick a couple into promising their baby. Marshall the raven realized this at once, but Tomlyn was deceived like Jarvis, the father, and thought he had promised a new-born puppy. Marshall loved the baby at sight. The witch had turned the deep well inside out and made it into a high tower. Marshall practised his restricted flying and went up to visit little Rapunzel. He became her devoted playmate, and though Tomlyn tried to preserve an indifferent air, he learned to fly by magic and visited her too. Little Rapunzel was a brilliant child, and by the time she was one year old the two familiars noticed that she was learning to work simple spells. There was no time to lose if they were to save the child from the dreadful fate of being trained as a witch. Tomlyn borrowed the witch's terrible book of spells and raised a troll from it, by whose aid he laid a spell on the baby so that no witchcraft would take on her. The witch became unable to teach her anything and by the time the child was three years old, she began to despair. In desperate impatience she summoned a consultant witch, who, after casting runes, delivered her opinion.

> If at one
> Nought's begun,
> Wait and see.
> Then, at three,
> Try again.
> Or at ten.
> At sixteen
> All serene –
> Or, if not,
> That's the lot!'[10]

Mother Gothel was impatient for another opinion, so she summoned a famous authority, a Highland White Wizard. Tomlyn saw him first.

> He appeared on the path, while I was having a scratch-up under a bush near by. Nearly jumped out of my skin! He raised his woollen cap to me, and said he was sorry in a soft, deep voice with a singing note to it. I said all right I'd seen him coming, and he said he'd noticed. He went and knocked on the cottage door. I found, to my surprise, that I was following close at his heels, and I turned to run away. It surprised me even more when I followed him right into the house, and into the parlour, and over to the fire, and sat down on the rug and stared at him.
>
> He was a queer one. He bowed to madam, but he didn't shake hands with her. Madam was furious. Yet she was impressed by him, you could see. He was big and tall, and handsome – as sorcerers go – and he had long, rust-coloured hair, and long, large hands. He sat down in the best chair, refused a cup of tea very firmly, and said what was the problem?
>
> Madam told him. She went on and on about the stupidness of Rapunzel – how magic wouldn't take on her – how she couldn't even remember a single word of witchcraft, though bright enough in other ways – and the wizard listened gravely. Suddenly, I saw his green eyes go narrow. He glanced sideways at me. Then I found to my horror that I'd crept nearer and nearer to him, without noticing what I was doing, and he put his hand on my head. I leapt away, and shot under the sofa, swearing.
>
> 'I like cats,' he said.[11]

Tomlyn was terrified at this, sure that the wizard had seen through all their plans, would betray them and counteract the spell they had cast on little Rapunzel. The wizard said nothing to betray them, however, merely referred to Mrs Hagadin's consultation – which Mother Gothel had not intended to mention, and told her to obey the runes, test the child from time to time, and wait patiently till she was sixteen. He bowed farewell and asked for the escort of Mother Gothel's fine puss-cat to the gate.

Tomlyn refused to go but he went for all that. When they got outside the gate the wizard invited Tomlyn to go with him, telling him what a dangerous game he was playing for the sake of the child and of the raven. Tomlyn spat and snarled and said he played for laughs. He was sure the wizard was luring him, laying a love-spell on him, and he struck out at him, only with carefully sheathed claws. The wizard told him where he lived and that his name was Macpherson, and advised him to seek him when the need came. Then he set Tomlyn down and vanished.

The years passed on, Rapunzel became more beautiful and increasingly dearer to the two familiars. Marshall contrived to visit her parents and carry messages to and fro. But the fatal sixteenth birthday grew nearer and the witch more frantic with impatience. At length the fearful day came when the witch began to bake the sinister birthday cake. There was no more time to wait, and Tomlyn set off upon the perilous journey to the mountains and the pinewood where Macpherson had his home, and from him obtained the spell which brought the Prince to Rapunzel. The story after that follows the outline of Grimm's fairytale except that the desert where Rapunzel and the Prince found each other is the desolate far side of the moon, and old Marshall is the agent who procures the happy ending. Tomlyn still trying to demonstrate his toughness, yet stays by the witch and disenchants her in the end. The last words of the book show Tomlyn still in character.

'Cheeky old wizard! I could spit!' said he.
He spat.[12]

Over the Hills to Fabylon is another book by Nicholas Stuart Gray in which the cats play a considerable part. It is a string of episodes threaded together to make a complete plot. All the cats of Fabylon play their part in the story. There is Courteney, the Princess's stately pet, the much indulged pair in the Apothecary's household and a neat little witch cat who had once been Wildfire Winnie, a human witch, but preferred the quieter life of a cat, and now practised under the name of Serena; it takes most of the cats of the city to rescue Princess Rosetta from The Glow-worm caves.[13] This is the lightest of Nicholas Stuart Gray's books, but is full of anecdotes of wizardry and magic and of supernatural creatures, some invented and some true to folk tradition.

C. S. Lewis is another author who uses mythology and folklore significantly and with fundamental respect. His world of Narnia, though its morals are universal to all worlds, has one particular in which it differs from Earth: in the first day of Narnia some animals acquired souls and became Talking Beasts.[14] If they betrayed this privilege a terrible punishment might fall on them – they might lose it for ever. In the final book of the Narnia series, *The Last Battle*,[15] this punishment falls upon a cat, who inherits the sly and intriguing tendencies which, as we have seen, are so often attributed to the cat in folk legends. He allies himself with an ape called Shift and with Narnia's hereditary enemies, the Calormenes, to dress up an innocent puzzle-headed donkey as Aslan the Lion (the Christ figure of the books) and dominate Narnia. The demon–idol Tash is called Tashlan and impiously compounded with Aslan. The creatures are dared to go one by one into the stable where the donkey was hidden. It is secretly arranged that the cat shall accept the challenge and bring back false evidence. He brings a weightier evidence than the conspirators expected. The loyalists, hiding in the shadow of the stable, see what happened.

> Then a most surprising thing happened. Ginger the Cat said in a cool, clear voice, not at all as if he was excited. 'I'll go in, if you like.'
>
> Every creature turned and fixed its eyes on the Cat. 'Mark their subtleties, Sire,' said Poggin to the King. 'This cursed cat is in the plot, in the very centre of it. Whatever is in the Stable will not hurt him, I'll be bound. Then Ginger will come out again and say that he has seen some wonder.'

And the Cat got up and came out of its place in the crowd, walking primly and daintily, with its tail in the air, not one hair on its sleek coat out of place. It came on till it had passed the fire and was so close that Tirian, from where he stood with his shoulder against the end-wall of the stable, could look right into its face. Its big green eyes never blinked. ('Cool as a cucumber,' muttered Eustace. 'It knows it has nothing to fear.') The Ape, chuckling and making faces, shuffled across beside the Cat: put up his paw: drew the bolt and opened the door. Tirian thought he could hear the Cat purring as it walked into the dark door-way.

'Aii–aii–aouwee! –' The most horrible caterwaul you ever heard made everyone jump . . . .

The Ape was knocked head over heels by Ginger coming back out of the Stable at top speed. If you had not known he was a cat, you might have thought he was a ginger-coloured streak of lightning. He shot across the open grass, back into the crowd. No one wants to meet a cat in that state. You could see animals getting out of his way to left and right. He dashed up a tree, whisked round, and hung head downwards. His tail was bristled out till it was nearly as thick as his whole body: his eyes were like saucers of green fire: along his back every single hair stood on end.[16]

He had become a dumb beast. He plainly tried to say words, but he could only wawl. At length he disappeared up the tree and was not seen again.

It is rather sad that this is the most explicit picture that C. S. Lewis gives us of a cat, for he loved all animals. But their elegance and the air of sophistication about them makes them tempting models for a villain.

Andrew Lang, in one of his few original fairy stories, throws a more affectionate and sympathetic eye upon a cat. Old Frank is a small strand in the story, but a loving glance is cast upon him. The tale is *Prince Prigio*, and it is to be found in *My Own Fairy Book*,[17] a collection of three short stories, the first two modelled on the sophisticated French fairytales, of the visit of the fairies (one of whom is malevolent) to a royal baby's christening with magical gifts. The King's eldest little son, Prince Prigio, is given all manner of magical gifts by the ninety-nine good fairies who attend his christening; the ill-natured hundredth fairy lays a curse on him: 'My child you shall be too clever.'

This gift caused him, as he grew up, to be more and more unpopular, hated by everyone but his mother, who was as clever as he was, far too clever to believe in fairy gifts. In fact on the very day of the christening she had them all swept away into the attic –

shoes of swiftness, cap of darkness, sword of sharpness and all –
where they lay forgotten until the Prince, left alone in the summer
palace by his angry father and the scoffing courtiers, finds and
puts some of them on to replace his own wardrobe, which has
been wantonly destroyed. Even then he cannot understand the
strange things that happen to him until he falls in love, and then he
understands in a flash, and realizes that there really is such a
monster as the Firedrake and that his two younger brothers went
to their death in a vain attempt to destroy it. Prigio, by the adroit
use of his magical properties and his superior intelligence, destroys
the Firedrake, but his more difficult task is to restore his brothers
to life. He experiments on an old cat, the sole inhabitant of the
castle which has been deserted by the court.

How still it was, how deserted; not a sign of life, and yet the
prince was looking everywhere *for some living thing*. He
hunted the castle through in vain, and then went out to the
stable-yard; but all the dogs, of course, had been taken away,
and the farmers had offered homes to the poultry. At last,
stretched at full length in a sunny place, the prince found a
very old, half-blind, miserable cat. The poor creature was
lean, and its fur had fallen off in patches; it could no longer
catch birds, nor even mice, and there was nobody to give it
milk. But cats do not look far into the future; and this old
black cat – Frank was his name – had got a breakfast somehow, and was happy in the sun. The prince stood and looked
at him pityingly, and he thought that even a sick old cat was,
in some ways, happier than most men.

'Well,' said the prince at last, 'he could not live long any-
way, and it must be done. He will feel nothing.'

Then he drew the sword of sharpness, and with one turn
of his wrist cut the cat's head clean off.

Then the prince built up a heap of straw, with wood on it;
and there he laid poor puss, and set fire to the pile. Very
soon there was nothing of old black Frank left but ashes!

Then the prince ran upstairs to the fairy cupboard, his
heart beating loudly with excitement. The sun was shining
through the arrow-shot window; all the yellow motes were

dancing in its rays. The light fell on the strange heaps of fairy things – talismans and spells. The prince hunted about here and there, and at last he discovered six ancient water-vessels of black leather, each with a silver plate on it, and on the plate letters engraved. This was what was written on the plates:

AQUA. DE. FONTE. LEONUM.

'Thank heaven!' said the prince. 'I thought they were sure to have brought it!'

Then he took one of the old black-leather bottles, and ran downstairs again to the place where he had burned the body of the poor old sick cat.

He opened the bottle, and poured a few drops of the water on the ashes and the dying embers.

Up there sprang a tall, white flame of fire, waving like a tongue of light; and forth from the heap jumped the most beautiful strong, funny, black cat that ever was seen!

It was Frank as he had been in the vigour of his youth; and he knew the prince at once, and rubbed himself against him and purred.

The prince lifted up Frank and kissed his nose for joy; and a bright tear rolled down on Frank's face, and made him rub his nose with his paw in the most comical manner.

Then the prince set him down, and he ran round and round after his tail; and, lastly, cocked his tail up, and marched proudly after the prince into the castle.

'Oh, Frank!' said Prince Prigio, 'no cat since the time of

Puss In Boots was ever so well taken care of as you shall be. For if the fairy water from the fountain of Lions can bring you back to life – why, there is a chance for Alphonso and Enrico!'[18]

A very different kind of cat was Sam in Walter de la Mare's *Broomsticks*,[19] who, after being a faithful companion to Miss Chauncey for some four years, was seduced by a coven of witches, betrayed his allegiance and turned her house into a haunt of witchcraft. The atmosphere is built up by a hundred subtle touches, as de la Mare well knows how. The story is not long, and must be read in its entirety. The mark of a broomstick deep in the ground, the swish of a spent rocket, the frou-frou of a stiff silk gown – 'She never noticed such things without being instantly transported back in imagination to her bedroom at Post Houses, and seeing again that strange deluded animal, once her Sam, squatting there on her bed, and as it were knitting with his fore-paws the while he stood erect upon his hind.'[20]

The heroine of *Miss Kelly*,[21] by Elizabeth S. Holding, was an entirely admirable cat and extremely intelligent. It is a story of modern American life. The only folklore element in it is the animals' ability to talk, a faculty developed by the brilliant intelligence of Miss Kelly, who finds it possible to teach it to her more receptive friends among the animals. Miss Kelly was the daughter of two very intelligent parents. She learnt something about the meaning of words from her mother, but she developed the power of speech entirely on her own initiative.

Miss Kelly's mother had been thoughtful and sensitive. She had taught all her kittens to understand the few Human words most important to know. The first was *cat*, so that they would know if they were being talked about, then *milk* and *fish* and *mouse* and *like* and *don't like*, and others. Miss Kelly's mother had never said anything about learning to speak the words, though, and when one day her daughter, after long, secret practising, said very proudly, 'Like fish,' she was greatly alarmed.

'Never do that again, child!' she had said. 'It's extremely dangerous.'

'Well, why?' the kitten had asked her.

'Never mind why,' her mother had answered. 'Just do as I tell you. Never let the Humans know you can understand them, and never, never let them hear you speak one single word.'[22]

On pertinacious questioning her mother explained that her father had led a life of misery because he was too intelligent, and she realized that she must keep her power secret, though she could not help teaching her neighbours the meaning of human words. One day, however, self-expression was forced on her.

One day a young tiger escaped from a circus. He was an intelligent but most embittered animal, who had been captured as a cub and had been too proud to learn the tricks that were forced on him. His sole object had been to kill all the humans he could reach and to escape back to the jungles of India. He broke open the door of the Clinton's and struck down the servant girl, Janet, of whom Miss Kelly was very fond. Terrified but brave, Miss Kelly advanced and accosted the tiger. After some argument she persuaded him to follow her to a little wood where she hid him for the night, promising to fetch him food in the morning. All night she taught him the meaning of human words, and in the morning she went home to find some food. She was received with rapture by the family. Some journalists arrived to take photographs, and from their talk she learned that the tiger had been captured and taken to a newly opened zoo because the circus thought him unteachable. She realized that the Tiger Prince would believe that she had betrayed him. She must go to him in the zoo to help him, but she could only do it by human aid. There was no help for it but for her to break her taboo. She went into the dining room where Mr Clinton was alone, glancing through the paper. Miss Kelly jumped up into Mrs Clinton's empty chair.

'Excuse me, Mr Clinton,' she said and knew that her voice was faint and unsteady.

'Excuse me, Mr Clinton, please take me to the Whitebrook Zoo.'[23]

There is one traditional assumption in this story which is that animals have human reason and organs capable of human speech. Its little heroine is one of the most charming in literature.

In children's nursery tales it is generally assumed that animals are capable of human skills and dexterity, so it is not surprising to find this assumed in Beatrix Potter's books, for she is more capable than any other artist of making animals look natural and dignified in human clothes, but *The Tailor of Gloucester* contains other folklore elements as well as the almost universal property, and its hero is a cat. The edition from which I quote is that most generally known, published in 1903. This more compact version is likely to be familiar to everyone and the little changes made in it have produced a more rhythmic and poetic style. It is a masterpiece and deserves to be read every Christmas Day. The old belief, that all animals can talk in human speech at midnight on Christmas Eve, is combined with a kind of embroidery of nursery rhymes as poor hungry Simpkin goes roaming through the snow.

But it is in the old story that all the beasts can talk, in the night between Christmas Eve and Christmas Day in the morning (though there are very few folk that can hear them, or know what it is that they say).

When the Cathedral clock struck twelve there was an answer – like an echo of the chimes – and Simpkin heard it, and came out of the tailor's door, and wandered about in the snow.

From all the roofs and gables and old wooden houses in Gloucester came a thousand merry voices singing the old Christmas rhymes – all the old songs that ever I heard of, and some that I don't know; like Whittington's bells.

First and loudest the cocks cried out 'Dame, get up and bake your pies!'

'Oh, dilly, dilly, dilly!' sighed Simpkin.

And now in a garret there were lights and sounds of dancing, and cats came from over the way.

'Hey, diddle, diddle, the cat and the fiddle! All the cats in Gloucester – except me,' said Simpkin.

Under the wooden eaves the starlings and sparrows sang of Christmas pies; the jackdaws woke up in the Cathedral tower; and although it was the middle of the night the throstles and robins sang; the air was quite full of little twittering tunes.

But it was all rather provoking for poor hungry Simpkin.

Particularly he was vexed with some little shrill voices from behind a wooden lattice. I think that they were bats, because they always have very small voices – especially in a black frost, when they talk in their sleep like the Tailor of Gloucester.

They said something mysterious that sounded like –

> 'Buzz, quoth the blue fly; hum, quoth the bee;
> Buzz and hum they cry, and so do we!'·

and Simpkin went away shaking his ears as if he had a bee in his bonnet.[24]

Then we have the episode of the little mice who are doing his work for the poor old sick tailor because he had rescued them from Simpkin.

From the tailor's shop in Westgate Street came a glow of light; and when Simpkin crept up to peep in at the window it was full of candles. There was a snippeting of scissors, and snappeting of thread; and little mouse voices sang loudly and gaily –

> 'Four-and-twenty tailors
> Went to catch a snail
> The best man amongst them
> Durst not touch her tail;
> She put out her horns
> Like a little kyloe cow,
> Run, tailors, run or she'll have you all e'en now!'

Then without a pause the little mouse voices went on again –

> 'Sieve my lady's oatmeal,
> Grind my lady's flour,
> Put it in a chestnut,
> Let it stand an hour –'

'Mew! Mew!' interrupted Simpkin, and he scratched at the door. But the key was under the tailor's pillow, he could not get in.

The little mice only laughed and tried another tune.

'Three little mice sat down to spin,
Pussy passed by and she peeped in
What are you at my fine little men?
Making coats for gentlemen,
Shall I come in and cut off your threads?
Oh, no, Miss Pussy, you'd bite off our heads!'[25]

And so they go on working and singing, until suddenly they jump up crying, 'No more twist!' and close the shutters, barring Simpkin out.

We, to whom the English language and literature belong, are fortunate in our children's books, and this is one of the best. Perhaps because of the excellent standard of the children's books written in English, from the nineteenth century onwards, grown-up readers have developed a taste for children's books out of which has gradually evolved a group of adult books founded on whimsy. The grim subject of witchcraft has been treated in this way, even from Ruddigore onwards. Stella Benson's *Living Alone*, a characteristic mixture of tragedy and humour, is an early example, written in the time of the First World War. The witch is the type of an artist, full of a detached, impersonal kindness but incurably irresponsible by worldly standards. She does not, however, come within the scope of our subject for her only familiar is Harold the Broomstick, a devoted servant, who would not cast so much as a glance aside at Satan himself, if he should appear.

Sylvia Townsend Warner, however, in *Lolly Willowes*,[26] introduces a most convincing familiar, a fierce, skinny, starving little kitten. His introduction to his new mistress seems almost fortuitous, for there is a careful casualness about the story which leaves one almost doubtful whether the witchcraft incidents occurred only in Laura Willowes's mind, just as people have maintained that the sinister tragedy in *The Turn of the Screw* was the product of Miss Sullivan's crazed imagination. In neither book, however, is the reader really left in doubt. Lolly Willowes, a born solitary, made desperate at the burden of aunthood thrust on her shoulders by her conventionally affectionate family, cried out suddenly in the loneliness of a wood for help from the forces of magic and was answered by a silence so massive that it gradually shaped itself in her mind into an acquiescence in her wish. She went half-unconscious home in the deepening dusk and was received by a meal laid ready for her that seemed part of the acquiescence. She felt that the very dishes on the table were fore-warned to be there. The scene was set for the arrival of a familiar.

As she spoke, she felt something move by her foot. She glanced down and saw a small kitten. It crouched by her foot, biting her shoe-lace, and lashing its tail from side to side. Laura did not like cats; but this creature, so small, so intent, and so ferocious, amused her into kindly feelings. 'How did you come here? Did you come in through the keyhole?' she asked, and bent down to stroke it. Scarcely had she touched its hard little head when it writhed itself round her hand, noiselessly clawing and biting, and kicking with its hind legs. She felt frightened by an attack so fierce and irrational, and her fears increased as she tried to shake off the tiny weight. At last she freed her hand, and looked at it. It was covered with fast-reddening scratches, and as she looked she saw a bright round drop of blood ooze out from one of them. Her heart gave a violent leap, and seemed to drop dead in her bosom. She gripped the back of a chair to steady herself and stared at the kitten. Abruptly pacified, it had curled itself into a ball and fallen asleep. Its lean ribs heaved with a rhythmic tide of sleep. As she stared she saw its pink tongue flicker for one moment over its lips. It slept like a suckling.

Not for one moment did she doubt . . . . She, Laura Willowes, in England, in the year 1922, had entered into a compact with the Devil. The compact was made, and affirmed, and sealed with the round red seal of her blood.[27]

And so Lolly Willowes acquired her familiar, and freed herself for ever from the obligation to obey other people's consciences.

It is strange here, as it is in Walter de la Mare's brooding perceptions, to see the themes that have for so long been considered the province of the simple mind taken over into complexity. The sophisticated French fairy stories had given us some warning of it. Their note had been struck again in the modern children's fairy tales, by George Macdonald, by Mrs Nesbit, by A. A. Milne, and many another talented writer. The stories which had been first told in grown-up company had been long abandoned to the children, but now the grown-ups have recaptured their lost territory and with exquisite sophistication have dipped into fantasy.

APPENDIX 1

Traditions about Cats in the United States of America

Professor Wayland Hand of the Center for the Study of Comparative Folklore and Mythology in the University of California, Los Angeles, has very kindly made me these extracts from his massive Encyclopedia of American Folklore still in process of collection, and has most generously allowed me to quote them. It seemed more appropriate to keep them together rather than to scatter them through the book, so that the reader could gain access to the variety of opinions displayed and be conscious of the large area that they cover.

In doing so I should like to express my gratitude for the many kindnesses I have received from Professor Hand and from a great number of eminent scholars among the folklorists of America. I count it an especial honour to have been made an honorary member of The American Folklore Society.

29910   On Old Christmas Eve, all animals talk to spirits and get on their knees to pray (Mrs C.C., F, 37, farmw., Ir.-Du.-Gr., Crown City, 1956); . . . on Twelfth Night, all the animals in the stable will get on their knees (Mrs J.S., F, 40, secy., Ger., Wickliffe, 1956).

29911   It is said generally in southeastern Ohio that at the stroke of midnight on December thirty-first animals get down on their knees to welcome the New Year (B.H., M, 50, jour., Ger., Columbus, 1955).

29912   All domestic animals kneel to pray on New Year's Day (E.P., F, 30, h.wife, Negro, Cleveland, 1955).

29913   Animals kneel at midnight on St John's Eve and on Christmas Eve (M.S., F, 40, h.wife, Ger., Marshallville, 1958).

29914   A cat has seven lives (Mrs A.R., F, 81, farmw., Eng., Brunswick, 1956).

29915   A cat has nine lives (E.F., M, 65, army officer, Hung., Cleveland, 1963); . . . a black cat has nine lives (Mrs C.W., F, 50, h.wife, Ger., Cleveland, 1959).

29917 A cat has nine lives. For three he plays, for three he strays, and for the last three he stays (L.G., F, 13, Eng., Cleveland, 1955).

29918 All cats have nine lives, and therefore keep returning to life until it has nine deaths (W.L., M, 35, salesman, Ir., Cleveland, 1956).

29919 A cat can't be accepted in heaven or in hell until it uses all of its nine lives (Mrs M.F., F, 35, h.wife, Du., Cleveland, 1955).

29922 If you see a one-eyed cat, you will have bad luck unless you cross and uncross your fingers three times (J.K., M, 30, accountant, Ir., Cleveland, 1961).

29923 When you see a one-eyed cat, spit on your thumb, stamp it in the palm of your hand, and make a wish. The wish will come true (J.G., F, 25, h.wife, Fr.-Eng., Cleveland, 1962).

29924 A pink-eyed cat brings bad luck (R.K., M, 16, student, Cleveland, 1933).

29925 A calico cat, i.e. one with three colors, is the best kind of a cat to have (Mrs A.R., F, 81, farmw., Eng., Brunswick, 1956).

29926 Three-colored cats are always females (D.S., M, 50, equip. opr, Welsh-Eng., Jackson, 1957).

29927 If you see a three-colored cat, it's good luck (P.H., F, 22, nurse, Ger., Cleveland, 1963).

29928 Seeing a cat with fur in five colors will bring good luck (T.I., M, 45, ins. man, Croat., Cleveland, 1958).

29929 A white cat means good luck (W.J., M, 40, salesman, Ir.-Norw., Cleveland, 1955).

29930 Dreaming of a white cat means good luck (Mrs S., F, Eng., Madison, 1964).

29931 If a white cat comes to you, it is a sign of bad luck (Mrs R.N., F, Athens, 1956).

29932 A white cat is unlucky (Mrs O., F, 60, prof. baby sitter, Eng.-Ir., Cleveland, 1958).

29933 It is bad luck when you see a white cat at night (C.H., F, Farmersville, 1956).

29934 A white cat, especially if it has six toes, is a sign of good luck (E.I., F, 70, h.wife, Eng.-Scot., Cleveland, 1961).

29935 A black cat is good luck (Mrs M.M., F, 50, h.wife, Eng., Cleveland, 1957); . . . a black cat is lucky (Mrs O., F, 70, prof. baby sitter, Eng.-Ir., Cleveland, 1958); . . . to an Englishman a black cat means good luck (T.B., M, 17, student, Cleveland, 1956); . . . in Scotland a black cat is a sign of good luck (J.M., F,

16, student, Scot., Wickliffe, 1956); . . . to see a black cat means good luck (M.B., F, 50, Ger., Cleveland, 1955).

29936   Never get the illwill of a black cat (F.S., M, 55, Ir., Cleveland, 1955).

29938   It is bad luck to see a black cat (A.F., M, 81, farmer, Ger., Oceola, 1956); . . . it is bad luck to see a black cat before break-fast (Mrs M.V., F, 60, seamstress, Hung., Cleveland, 1958); . . . it is bad luck when you see a black cat in the daytime (C.H., F, Farmersville, 1956).

29939   If you see a black cat at night, walk away, or you'll have bad luck (Mrs M.M., F, 53, h.wife, Scot., Cleveland, 1962).

29940   If you see a black cat, spit three times at it and you won't have bad luck (Mrs J.P., F, 50, h.wife, Swed., Cleveland, 1960).

29941   When you see a black cat, turn around seven times, or you will have bad luck (A.H., F, 42, Eng.-Scot.-Ir., Dayton, 1955).

29943   To ward off bad luck from superstitions, like seeing a black cat, wet your index finger, press it on your palm, and then slap your palm three times with your fist (P.C., F, 55, secy, Ir., Paines-ville, 1965).

29944   It's bad luck for a black cat to rub up against you (S.B., F, 55, maid, Negro-Ind., Cleveland, 1958).

29945   When a black cat is sleeping, be sure that you don't awake it. If you do, everything will go wrong that month (Mrs K.L., F, 22, student, Ger., Rocky River, 1957).

29946   The sneezing of a cat is a good omen for all who hear it (M.A., F, 19, student, It., Cleveland, 1958).

29948   A black cat going to the left means bad luck (A.H., F, 45, nurse's aide, Negro, Cleveland, 1957).

29949   If a black cat comes to you, it will bring good luck (Mrs R.N., F, Athens, 1956); . . . if a black cat follows you, etc. (E.A., F, 16, Lith., Cleveland, 1933).

29951   Don't you see we were very superstitious or I never would of remembered all these. Now here's one worse to tell, but all goes when I get started. When a cat is washing under her tail, grab her leg that is up in the air and make a wish. (Mrs A.R., F, 81, farmw., Eng., Brunswick, 1955).

29953   In the interpretation of a dream, cats mean craftiness (Mrs M.M., F, 57, h.wife, Hung., Cleveland, 1958).

29954   The reason there are so many superstitions about cats is because they are not mentioned in the Bible (Mrs M.R., F, 57, h.wife, Ger.-Ir., Lakewood, 1958).

29955   If a man makes up with a cat and likes the cat, he will always have luck (Mrs M.S., F, 49, h.wife and pract. nurse, Penn.Ger., Lakewood, 1958).

29956 Dictators hate cats (Mrs J.R., F, 26, tech., Scot.-Ir., Cleveland, 1961).

29958 Tomcats, when they fight, talk English and swear at one another (K.M., M, lawyer, Ger., Bowling Green, 1956).

29959 If a dog chases a cat up a tree in the light of a new moon, something bad will happen (W.D., F, 15, student, Ger., Belpre, 1958).

29961 Because of a cat's 'sometimes sneaky way,' some people believe a cat will mate with unrelated animals like racoons, skunks, or rabbits (S.F., M, 48, loader, It., Cleveland, 1958).

29962 A cat has the number of kittens – also the same color – one for each male with whom she was intimate (Mrs C.C., F, 37, farmw., Ir.-Du.-Ger., Crown City, 1956).

29967 If you sleep with a cat, its tail will go down your throat (W.D., M, 28, eng., Ger., Cleveland, 1956).

29969 If scared by a cat, collect hair from a cat or dog, and burn it under your nose (K.B., M, 45, paperhanger, Lith., Cleveland, 1956).

29970 Never stroke a cat backward, or your luck will turn bad (F.U., F, office worker, Yugosl., Cleveland, 1959); . . . the informant's Pennsylvania-Dutch mother told her that if you stroke a cat the wrong way, it creates a catastrophe (J.B., F, Columbus, 1925).

29973 To step over a cat brings bad luck (J.M., F, student, Cleveland, 1925).

29974 If you harm a cat, you will have misfortune (A.B., M, 30, scient., Russ., Cleveland, 1962).

29979 If a cat comes to your home and won't leave it, it will bring good luck if taken in (A.M., F, 55, clerk, Sloven., Euclid, 1958).

29980 It's good luck if a black cat comes to your house (B.B., M, 66, ret., Ger., Cleveland, 1961); . . . a black cat visiting one's house means good luck (anon. Defiance Co., 1938, microf.); . . . a black cat entering a house voluntarily brings very good fortune (V.K., F, 44, h.wife, and student, Eng.-Scot.-Can., Cleveland, 1955).

29984 A strange cat is supposed to bring good fortune to the house in which it makes its home (anon. Montgomery Co., 1938, microf.); . . . if a stray cat comes to your house and stays there, it will bring good luck (LM., M, 58, machinist, Ir.-Du., Canton, 1956); . . . when a stray cat comes to your door, you must never turn it away, but keep it (R.A., F, Ger., Cleveland,

1933); . . . if a stray cat comes to your home, keep it for good luck (L.P., F, 45, servant, Negro, Cleveland 1955); . . . if a stray cat comes in your house, be kind to it, and you will have good luck (E.A., F, 88, h.wife, Eng., Paulding, 1961).

29985 Although black cats are considered to be unlucky, a stray cat, especially a black one, which makes its home with a person, will bring the person good luck (R.M., F, 20, student, Pol., Cleveland, 1961); . . . if a black cat comes to your door, take it in, etc. (P.M., F, 45, Welsh–Ger., East Greenville, 1965).

29989 If a black cat comes to your home, do not chase it away. If it leaves of its own accord, it will take bad luck with it. If you chase it, it will leave bad luck (Mrs M.R., F, 57, h.wife, Ger.-Ir., Lakewood, 1958).

29991 If a calico cat comes to your door, you will have good luck (Mrs M.V., F, 49, h.wife, Hung., Warren, 1958); . . . three-colored cats were good luck. Many a three-colored cat was rounded up and set in our front vestibule entrance by me or my friends. Mother would exclaim on opening the door, 'A three-colored cat has come to us!' I would always get to keep it. (A.M., F, Cleveland, 1955).

29992 If a black cat comes to your door, bad luck. The blacker the cat, the blacker the luck (A.M., F, Cleveland, 1955).

29996 A cat on the doorstep in the morning means bad luck (J.B., M, 25, student, Norw., Parma, 1965).

29997 A strange black cat on your porch brings prosperity (Mrs J.B., F, 41, h.wife, Scot., Cleveland, 1956).

29999 It's bad luck to put the cat out before you wind the clock (Mrs J.E., F, 66, h.wife, Welsh, Cleveland, 1956).

30000 Letting a cat look into a mirror will cause you trouble (Mrs C.C., F, 37, farmw., Ir.-Du-Ger., Crown City, 1956).

30004 It is bad luck to kill a cat (Mrs N.G., F, 68, school patrolwoman, Barberton, 1957); . . . I wouldn't want to do anything mean to a cat, because I think that things happen to you if you do. It is really bad luck to kill one. (Mrs D.C., F, 70, businesswoman, Eng.-Ger., Columbus, 1957); . . . whoever kills a cat will never have good luck (anon. M, 56, laborer, Bohem., Gallipolis, 1958).

30006 It is bad luck to kill a cat, but if you drown them, you're all right. I had to drown a good many of them when I was a kid, for it was bad luck to get rid of them any other way. (T.S., M, 64, teacher, Scot.-Ir., Norwalk, 1956); . . . drowning kittens was bad luck. The job was always left to my father. However, he got around it nicely by waiting too long – or until their eyes were open – then they were too adorable to think of drowning (A.M., F, Cleveland, 1955).

30007   Colored people believe that it is good luck to boil a black cat alive (M.K., F, student, Cleveland, 1925).

30009   If you kill a cat, you will have seven years of bad luck (J.W., M, 30, laborer, Ir., Cleveland, 1956); . . . seven years of trouble (Mrs N.M., F, 64, h.wife, Negro, Cleveland, 1958).

30011   To kill a cat brings seventeen years of bad luck (W.W., M, 80, Ir., Belmont, 1955).

30013   If you kill a cat, you must bury it by the light of the moon, or it will come back and haunt you (D.S., M, 20, student, Ger., Cincinnati, 1955).

30014   If you bury a black cat at night while making a wish, the wish will come true (M.N., F, 16, Bohem., Cleveland, 1933).

30016   If you tie paper around all four paws of a cat, it will dance itself to death (Mrs C.C., F, 37, Farmw., Ir.-Du.-Ger., Crown City, 1956).

31168   A dog will get up many times a night to save his master, but a cat will get up just as many times to kill his master (M.S., F, 40, h.wife, Ger., Marshallville, 1958).

31170   Singing cats and whistling girls come to a bad end (D.S., F, 21, student, Ger.-Ir., Cleveland, 1957).

31172   If you get a cat and want it to stay, fetch it home at night (Mrs G.A., F, 53, Ger., Cleveland, 1933).

31173   If you put a kitten under the cover of your bed and wait until it crawls out himself, it will never leave you (G.B., M, 47, social worker, Negro, Cleveland, 1958).

31174   To keep a cat at home, put a piece of food under your armpit and give it to him to eat (J.K., M, 63, farmer, Ger.-Old Order Amish, Fredericksburg, 1957).

31176   If a strange cat licks butter from your fingers, the cat will remain with you (Mrs N.N., F, 41, Eng.-Bohem., Cleveland, 1955).

31178   To keep a cat home, butter its feet (Mrs C.R., F, 55, cook, New Riegel, 1957); . . . rub butter on a cat's paw to make her stay at home (T.S., M, 64, teacher, Scot.-Ir., Norwalk, 1956); . . . if you grease a cat's paws with butter, it will never go away (V.L., M, Quaker, Toledo, 1958); . . . to keep a cat from running away, put butter on its paws. The cat will lick off the butter and stay (Mrs R.B., F, Penn.Ger., Columbiana, 1929, Roninger, p.79); . . . if a cat persists in running away, you can stop it by putting butter on its paws (Mrs G.A., F, 53, Ger., Cleveland, 1933).

31179 Put butter on your cat's paws when you move, and the cat will never go back to the old house, but stay with you (P.H., F, 22, nurse, Ger., Cleveland, 1963); . . . grease a cat's four paws with butter, and you can move it to any new home. If it once starts to lick even one paw, it will never go back to its old home (Mrs M.S., F, 55, librarian, Eng.-Swiss, Cleveland, 1955); . . . when moving from one home to another, put lots of butter on pet cat's paws to let her know she is to stay. By the time she has it all licked off clean, she is settled in (Mrs I.C., F, 62, Bohem, Jefferson, 1964).

31186 If a stray cat comes to your house and you want her to stay, put some fur from its tail under the doorsill, and she will stay (Mrs M.S., F, 40, h.wife, Croat., Cleveland, 1956).

31192 When moving to a new home, always put the cat through the window instead of through the door. Then it will not leave (Mrs V.B., F, 60, social worker, Ger., Dayton, 1956).

31193 If a cat looks in a mirror and gets lost, it will find its way back home (Mrs E.O., F, 43, h.wife, Hung., Cleveland, 1961).

31197 When you move from one dwelling place to another, never carry your cat in your arms. Put him in a suitcase so he can't see where he is being taken, otherwise he will always go back to his old home (C.J., F, 35, policewoman, Dan., Cleveland, 1956).

31198 If a mother cat has a litter of kittens of uneven number, it will bring bad luck into the house that the cat belongs to (V.K., M, 40, lay-out man, Polish, Cleveland, 1955).

31199 One should throw away the first offspring of a female cat, because they all turn out bad (M.G., M, 39, teacher, It., Cincinnati).

31201 If you touch kittens before their eyes are open, the mother cat will let them starve (R.., M, 80, M.D., Ger., Toronto, 1958); . . . the mother cat will desert the kitten (Mrs G.A., F, 53, Ger., Cleveland, 1933).

31209 If you lose your pets like cats, sing to the grandaddy,* 'Grandaddy, Grandaddy, which way did they go?' It will tell you by wiggling and pointing its legs (Mrs M.M., F., 64, H.wife, Negro, Cleveland, 1958).

The numbers in the Appendix refer to Professor Hand's Encyclopedia of American Folklore which is still in preparation.

* Daddy Longlegs.

APPENDIX 2

Stories quoted and cited

The Big Cat and the Big Rat O'Sullivan, Sean, *Folktales of Ireland*,
Folktales of the World, Gen. ed. Dorson, R. M., Chicago, 1966.
p. 189.
Motif B.524.1.3 Cat kills attacking rat.
　　　B.871.1.6 Giant cat.
Chapter Two.

Black Annis Billson, C. J., *County Folklore of Leicestershire*, County
Folk-Lore 3, F.L.S., London, 1895, pp. 4–9.
Chapter One.

Black Annis Tongue, R. L., *Forgotten Folk Tales of the English
Counties*, London, 1970, p. 68.
Motif D.672　Obstacle flight.
Chapter One.

The Black Cat Buchan, Peter, *Ancient Scottish Tales*, Norwood
Editions, reprinted from *Transactions of the Buchan Field Club*, Peter-
head, 1908, p. 51.
Type 326　　　Variant to learn fear.
Motif H.141.12　Staying in a haunted house infested by cats.
　　　E.281　　Ghosts haunt house.
Chapter Nine.

'Cake Burns' (Auld Betty of Halifax) Henderson, W., *Notes on
the Folk-Lore of the Northern Counties of England and the Borders*,
F.L.S., London, 1879, p. 209.
Motif G.211.1.7　Witch in form of cat.
　　　D. 1741　Drawing blood of witch annuls spells.
Chapter Seven.

The Cat and the Crab Seki, Keigo, *Folktales of Japan*, Folktales of
the World, Gen. ed. Dorson, R. M., Chicago, 1963.
Type 275　The race of the fox and the crayfish.
Motif K.11.2　Race won by deception.
Chapter Four (summarized).

The Cat and the Dog   Zong-in-Sob, *Folktales from Korea*, Folktales of the World, Gen. ed. Dorson, R. M., Chicago, 1952.
Type 200 D   Why cat is indoors and dog outside in the cold.
Motif A.2133.3.1.1   Why cat keeps chimney corner.
      A.2133.3.2   Dog's characteristic haunt.
Chapter Three.

The Cat and the Mouse   Halliwell, J. O., *Nursery Rhymes and Nursery Tales of England*, London, n.d., p. 154.
Type 111   Cat and mouse converse. Cat eats mouse.
Motif K.561.1.1   Cat fails to be beguiled into releasing mouse.
Chapter Three.

The Cat and Mouse in Partnership   *Grimm's Fairy Tales* edited by James Stern, London, 1948, p. 21.
Type 15   Theft of butter.
Motif K.372   Playing godfather.
Chapter Three.

The Cat and the Mouse in the Public House   Murphy, M. J., *Now You're Talking*, Belfast, 1975, p. 224.
Type IIIA   A drunkard's promise.
Chapter Three.

The Cat Sisters   Owen, E., *Welsh Folk-Lore*, Norwood Editions, 1973, Oswestry, 1896, p. 224.
Motif G.211.1.7   Witch in form of cat.
      G.275.12   Witch in form of animal is injured by wounding of animal.
Chapter Seven.

The Cat's Allotment   Dov Noy, *Folktales of Israel*, Folktales of the World, Gen. ed. Dorson, R. M., Chicago, 1963, p. 64.
Motif A.2435.3.2   Food of cat
Chapter Two.

The Cat's Baptism   Wolkstein, D., *The Magic Orange Tree and Other Haitian Tales*, New York, 1978, p. 123.
Chapter Two.

The Cat's Elopement   Lang, Andrew, *The Pink Fairy Book*, London, 1936, translated from Braune, David, *Japanische Märchen und Sagen*, p. 1.
Type 130 (variant)   Animals go a-journeying.
Chapter Two.

The Cat's Only Trick   Murphy, M. J., *Now You're Talking*, Belfast, 1975, p. 140.
Type 105   The cat's only trick.

Motif J.1662 She saves herself on a tree. The fox, who knows a hundred tricks, is captured.

Chapter Four.

The Cattie in the Kiln-Ring Chambers, R., *Popular Rhymes of Scotland*, London & Edinburgh, 1870, p. 53.

Type 111 The cat and the mouse converse. Cat eats mouse.

Motif K.561.1.1 Cat fails to be beguiled into releasing mouse.

Chapter Eleven.

The Cat who Became Head-Forester Ransome, A., *Old Peter's Russian Tales*, London, 1933, p. 92.

Type 103 A The cat who became she-fox's husband.

Motif B.281.9.1 Cat becomes vixen's husband. Frightens the other wild animals invited by vixen.

Chapter Two.

Cecus-Becus Berneusz Degh, L., *Folktales of Hungary*, Folktales of the World, Gen. ed. Dorson, R. M., Chicago, 1961, p. 192.

Type 103 Wild animals hide from unfamiliar animal.

Motif K.2324 Cat shrieks and frightened bear falls from tree.

Chapter Two.

The Colony of Cats Lang, A., *The Crimson Fairy Book*, London, 1935, p. 340.

Type 403 (variant) Kind and unkind.

Chapter Nine.

The Cottager and his Cat Lang, A., *The Crimson Fairy Book* (from *Islandische Märchen*), London, 1935, p. 174.

Type 1651 Whittington's cat.

Motif J.1931 Coins thrown into water. Only one rises, the rest are counterfeit.

F. 708.1 Land where cats are unknown.

N.411.1 Cat sold for a fortune.

Chapter Nine.

Crowhurst and his wife Simpson, J., *The Folklore of Sussex*, London, 1973, p. 70. Motif G.211.1.7 Witch in form of cat.

Chapter Seven.

The Curious Cat Briggs, K. M. and Tongue, R. L., *Folktales of England*, Folktales of the World, Gen. ed. Dorson, R. M., London, 1965, p. 106.

Type 105A Cat's curiosity.

1191 Dog on bridge (variant).

Motif M.210 Bargain with Devil.

Chapter Two.

Death of Macgillichallum of Raazay Stewart, W. Grant, *The Popular Superstitions and Festive Amusements of the Highlands of Scotland*, Edinburgh, 1823, p. 184.
Motif G.211.1.7 Witch in form of cat.
   G.269.8   Ship wrecked by witches.
Chapter Seven.

Dutch Courage Briggs, K. M., *A Dictionary of British Folktales in the English Language*, 4 vols, London, 1970, vol. II, p. 66.
Type 111A Drunk mouse challenges cat.
Chapter Three.

The End of Brer Anansi Iremonger, L., *West Indian Folk-tales*, London, 1956, p. 59.
Motif A.522.7   Spider as culture hero.
   B.16.6.4   Devastating spider.
   A.2494.1.7 Enmity between cat and spider.
Chapter Four.

The Four-Eyed Cat Briggs, K. M. and Tongue, R. L., *The Folktales of England*, Folktales of the World, Gen. ed. Dorson, R. M., London, 1965, p. 56.
Motif G.283.1.2.3 Witch raises wind to sink ship.
   G.211.1.7   Witch in form of cat.
Chapter Five.

The Four Friends Massignon, G., *Folktales of France*, Folktales of the World, Gen. ed. Dorson, R. M., Chicago, 1968, p. 179.
Type 130 (variant) Animals in night quarters.
Motif B.296   Animals go a-journeying.
   B.211.1.8   Speaking cat.
Chapter Four.

The Hare and the Stickly-backed Urchin Cowling, H., *The Dialect of Harkness*, Cambridge, 1915, p. 165.
Type 1074 Contest between man and ogre: race.
Motif K.11.1 Race won by deception.
Chapter Four.

The Grateful Animals and the Talisman Dawkins, R. M., *Modern Greek Folktales*, Oxford, 1953, p. 40.
Type 540   The magic ring.
Motif D.810   Magic object a gift.
   D.1470   Magic wishing object.
   B.360   Animals grateful for rescue from death.
   B.422   Helpful cat.
   K.431   Mouse with tail in mouth of sleeping thief makes him cough up swallowed ring.

K.2213   Treacherous wife.

D.2136.2   Castle magically transported.

D.882.1.1   Stolen magic object stolen back by helpful dog and cat.

Chapter Four.

The Helpful Animals Eberhard, W., *Folktales of China*, Folktales of the World, Gen. ed. Dorson, R. M., Chicago, 1965, p. 141.

Type 540   The magic ring, I, II, III, IV.

Motif D.810   Magic object a gift.

D.861   Magic object stolen.

D.882.1.1   Stolen magic object stolen back by helpful dog and cat.

Chapter Three.

The Heron, the Cat and the Bramble Own, E., *Welsh Folk-Lore*, Norwood Editions, 1973, reprint from 1896, p. 323.

Type 289 (variant)   Bat, diver and thorn bush.

Motif A.2275.5.3   Bush catches passer-by looking for clothes.

Chapter Four.

Jack and his Comrades Kennedy, P., *Legendary Fictions of the Irish Celts*, London, 1891, p. 4.

Type 130   Animals in night quarters.

Motif B.290   Animals go a-journeying.

N.779   Light seen from tree guides them to house.

K.335.1.4   Animals climbing on one another's back frighten thieves from house.

Chapter Four.

Judy Agrah Wilde, S., *Ancient Legends of Ireland*, 2 vols, London, 1887, vol. II, p. 15.

Motif B.181.1   Magic cat.

Chapter One.

King Arthur's fight with the Great Cat Wilde, S. *Ancient Legends of Ireland*, 2 vols, London, 1887, vol. II, p. 37.

Motif B.8171.1.6   Giant cat.

G.246   Devastating monster.

F.628.1.0.1   Strong man slays monster.

Chapter Ten.

The King of the Cats. I Hartland, E. S., *English Fairy and Folk Tales*, Walter Scott Press, Newcastle-on-Tyne, n.d., p. 126.

Type 113A   The King of the Cats is dead.

Motif F.982.2   Four cats carry coffin.

B.34a   Cat leaves house when report is made of death of one of his companions.

The King of the Cats. II   Wilde, S., *Ancient Legends of Ireland*,
2 vols, London, 1887, vol. II, p. 29.
The King of the Cats and the Bard
   Motif F.981.7   Saint kills King of Cats carrying off bard.
   Chapter One.
Kisa the Cat   Lang, A., *The Brown Fairy Book*, (Neiuslandischen
   Volksmärchen), London, 1904, p. 256.
   Motif B.313   Helpful animal enchanted person.
      D.700   Person disenchanted.
      D.1500.1.19.1   Magic salve restores severed feet.
      S.162   Mutilation, cutting off feet.
   Chapter Eight.
Lord Peter   Dasent, G. W., *Popular Tales from the Norse,* Edinburgh,
   1903, p. 295.
   Type 454 B   Puss in boots.
   Motif N.411.1.1   Cat sole inheritance.
      B.211.1.8   Speaking cat.
      B.500   Animal helps man to wealth and greatness.
      D.711   Disenchanted by decapitation.
   Chapter Seven.
Maggie Osborne   Aitken, Hannah, *A Forgotten Heritage*, Edinburgh,
   1974.
   Motif G.211.1.7   Witch in form of cat.
      G.275.12   Witch in form of animal is injured by wounding
                     of animal.
The Man who killed the wrong cat   Griffiths, 'The Heart of
   Down', *Ulster Tatler*, n.d.
   Motif G.246   Devastating monster.
      H.1174   Suitor test: slaying monster.
      F.628.1.0.1   Strong man slays monster.
   Chapter Ten.
Mary Haynes   Rawling, M., *The Folklore of the Lake District*,
   London, 1976, pp. 26–7.
   Motif G.225.3   Cat as servant of witch.
      G.268.10   Witch punishes person who incurs her ill-will.
      D.1812   Magic power of prophecy.
Mother Kemp   Barrett, W. H., *More Tales from the Fens*, London,
   1964, p. 111.
   Motif G.225   Witch's familiar.
      G.225.3   Cat as servant of witch.
      G.225.7   Magician's familiar a viper.
      G.263.4.0.1   Illness caused by curse of witch.

G.269.10.1   Witch kills person as punishment.
Chapter Six.
Mouse and Mouser   Jacobs, J., *English Fairy Tales*, London, 1890,
p. 48.
Type 2034   Mouse regains tail.
Motif Z.41.4   Mouse regains tail. (chain tale)
Chapter Eleven.
The Old Woman and the pig   Halliwell, J. O., *Rhymes and Nursery Tales of England*, London, n.d., p. 114.
Type 2034   The mouse regains its tail.
Motif Z.41.4   Mouse retains its tail. (chain tale)
Chapter Eleven.
A Plantation Witch   Harris, J. C., *Uncle Remus*, London, 1901,
p. 254.
Motif G.211.17   Witch in form of cat.
G.275.8.4   Witch killed (injured) by placing salt inside skin
when set aside.
Chapter Seven.
Puddy and the Mouse   Chambers, R., *Popular Rhymes of Scotland*,
Edinburgh, 1841 (new edition 1870), p. 55.
Motif B.234.1.1   Wedding of frog and mouse
Chapter Eleven.
Spinning Jenny   Barrett, W. H., *More Tales from the Fens*, London,
1964, p. 129.
Motif G.225   Witch's familiar.
D.2065   Magic insanity.
D.2061.2.4   Death by cursing.
Chapter Six.
Three Cats from the Cave of Cruachan   Henderson, G., *Survivals in Belief Among the Celts*, Glasgow, 1911, p. 108.
Motif B.184   Magic cats.
Motif B.871.10   Giant cat.
Chapter Ten.
Tibb's Cat and the Apple-Tree Man   Briggs, K. M. and Tongue,
R. L., *Folktales of England*, Folktales of the World, Gen. ed.
Dorson, R. M., London, 1965, p. 46.
Type 103 A   Cat's curiosity.
Motif N.815.0.1   Helpful tree spirit.
Chapter Two.
The Two Caskets   Thorpe, B., *Yule-Tide Stories*, Bohn Library,
London, 1884, pp. 97–112.
Type 480   Kind and Unkind. I, II, IV, V, VI, VII, VIII.

Motif S.31   Cruel stepmother.
    L.55   Stepdaughter heroine.
    B.350   Grateful animals.
    D.1658.1.5 Apple-tree grateful.
    H.1023.2   Carrying water in sieve.
    H.1023.6   Washing black wool white.
    L.220   Modest request best.
Chapter Nine.

Two Lost Babes   Chase, Richard, *Grandfather Tales*, USA, 1948, p. 162.
Type 327 (variant)
Motif S.301   Children abandoned.
    G.211.1.7   Witch in form of cat.
    G.270   Witch overcome or evaded.
Chapter Seven.

The White Cat   *Fairy Tales by the Countess d'Aulnoy*, translated by Planché, J. R., London, n.d. (circa 1911), p. 337.
Type 403   Cat as bride.
Motif H.1210.1   Quests assigned by father.
    H.1307   Quest for smallest dog.
    H.1306   Quest for the finest of linen.
    H.1301.1   Quest for the most beautiful bride.
    H.1242   Youngest brother succeeds.
    B.313   Helpful animal an enchanted person.
    D.711   Disenchantment by decapitation.
Chapter Eight.

The White Rat and the Cat   Porter, E., *The Folklore of East Anglia*, London, 1974, p. 148.
Motif A.2494.1.4 Enmity between cat and rat.
Chapter Two.

Whittington and his Cat   Hartland, E. S., *English Fairy and Folk Tales*, London, Walter Scott Ltd, n.d., p. 60.
Type 1651   Whittington's cat.
Motif N.708.1   The cat taken to mouse-infested land.
    N.411.13   Cat sold for a fortune.
Chapter Nine.

Why Dogs Dislike Cats and Cats Dislike Mice   Ratclif, R. *New Tales from Grimm*, Edinburgh, 1960, p. 27.
Type 200   The dog's certificate.
Motif A.2281.1 Cat loses dog's certificate.
Chapter Three.

The Witch of Laggan   Stewart, Grant, *The Popular Superstitions and Festive Amusements of the Highlanders of Scotland*, Edinburgh, 1825, p. 189.

Motif G.211.1.7	Witch in form of cat.
G.275.2	Witch overcome by helpful dogs of hero.
9303.3.1.7	Devil as a huntsman.
E.501.15.6	Behaviour of wild huntsman's dogs.

Chapter Seven.

Notes

Chapter 1   The Cult of the Cat and the Cat Goddess

1 Larousse *Encyclopedia of Mythology*, translated by Richard Aldington and Delano Ames, Batchworth Press, London, 1959. Egyptian Mythology, Bast, pp. 36 and pp. 46–8. See also Spence, Lewis, *Myths and Legends of Ancient Egypt*, London, 1917, p. 10.
2 *The Historian's History of the World*, 25 vols, William Henry Smith, 1904, vol. 1, p. 228.
3 Diodorus Siculus, a famous Roman historian, was born in Sicily in the first century BC. He wrote *The Historical Library*, a world history in 40 volumes, of which only I to V and XI to XX survive. A translation, *The Historical Library*, 1700, has never been supplanted.
4 Spence, Lewis, *The Myths and Legends of Ancient Egypt*, p. 293.
5 Ibid., pp. 188–9.
6 Ibid., pp. 148–50.
7 Grimm, Jacob, *Teutonic Mythology*, translated by J. S. Stallybrass, London, 1882, vol. I, pp. 304–6.
8 The story of Liban derives from a seventeenth-century work *The Annals of the Kingdom of Ireland* by The Four Masters. The full story is told by P. W. Joyce in *Old Celtic Romances*, London, 1894.
9 Mackenzie, D. A., *Scottish Folk-Lore and Folk Life*, London and Glasgow, 1935, pp. 137–8.
10 Ibid., pp. 130–1.
11 Ibid., p. 171.
12 Billson, C. J., *County Folk-Lore. Printed Extracts No. 3*, Leicestershire and Rutland, F.L.S., London, 1895: Black Annis's Bower, pp. 4–9.
13 Dudley, John, *Naology*, London, 1846, pp. 249–50.
14 *Leicester Chronicle*, in Billson, *County Folk-Lore*, p. 8.

15 Ibid., p. 9.
16 This is in a letter from Sir John Mellor to the Editor of the *Leicester Chronicle*, 7 November 1874, in Billson, pp. 8–9.
17 Tongue, R. L., *Forgotten Folk-Tales of the English Counties*, London, 1970, pp. 68–70.
18 Henderson, W., *Folk-Lore of the Northern Counties*, Folk Lore Society, London, 1879, p. 123.
19 Hartland, E. S., *English Fairy and Folk Tales*, Walter Scott Ltd, London, n.d. pp. 126–7; from the *Folk-Lore Journal*, II, London, 1884, p. 22.
20 Henderson, George, *Survivals in Belief Among the Celts*, Glasgow, 1911, pp. 267–9. Mackenzie, D. A., *Scottish Folk-Lore and Folk Life*, Glasgow, 1935, pp. 245–6.
21 Wilde, Speranza, *Ancient Legends, Mystic Charms and Superstitions of Ireland*, London, 1887, vol. II, p. 12.
22 Ibid., pp. 14–15.
23 Ibid., pp. 24–30.
24 Ibid., pp. 16–19.
25 Ibid., pp. 15–16.

Chapter 2   Feline Characteristics

1 Rackham, Arthur, *Mother Goose*, London, n.d.
2 Ibid., p. 126.
3 Halliwell, J. O., *Nursery Rhymes and Nursery Tales of England*, 5th edition, London, n.d., p. 101.
4 Ibid., p. 84.
5 Chambers, R., *Popular Rhymes of Scotland*, Edinburgh, 1870, p. 26.
6 *Medieval Lore*, selected from the writings of Bartholomew Anglicus by Robert Steele, London, 1905, p. 165.
7 Topsell, Edward, *The Historie of Four-Footed Beastes*, London, 1607, pp. 105 and 106.
8 Briggs, K. M. and Tongue, R. L., *Folktales of England*, Folktales of the World. Gen. ed., Dorson, R. M., London, 1965, pp. 105–6.
9 Ibid. pp. 46–7.
10 Dov, Noy, *Folktales of Israel*, Folktales of the World, Chicago, 1963, p. 64.
11 Ransome, Arthur, *Old Peter's Russian Tales*, London, 1935, pp. 92–104.
12 Degh, Linda, *The Folktales of Hungary*, Folktales of the World, Chicago, 1965, pp. 102–3.

13 O'Sullivan, Sean, *Folktales of Ireland*, Folktales of the World, Chicago, 1966, pp. 189–91.
14 Porter, Enid, *The Folklore of East Anglia*, London, 1974, p. 148.
15 Lang, A., *The Pink Fairy Book*, London, 1936, pp. 1–5, translated from *Japanische Märchen und Sagen*, by David Braune.
16 Volkstein, Diane, *The Magic Orange Tree and Other Haitian Folktales*, New York, 1978, pp. 123–6.

Chapter 3 Traditional Enemies

1 Michaelis Jena, R. and Ratcliff, A., *New Tales from Grimm*, Edinburgh, 1960, pp. 27–8.
2 Zong-in-Zob, *Folktales from Korea*, Folktales of the World, Chicago, 1952, pp. 25–31.
3 Eberhard, Wolfram, *Folktales of China*, Folktales of the World, Chicago, 1965, pp. 141–3.
4 *Grimms Fairy Tales*, edited by James Stern, London, 1948, pp. 21–3.
5 Murphy, M. J., *Now You're Talking*, Belfast, 1975, pp. 224–5.
6 Briggs, K. M., *A Dictionary of British Folktales in the English Language*, 4 vols, London, 1970, vol. II, p. 66, 'Dutch Courage'
7 Halliwell, J. O., *Nursery Rhymes and Nursery Tales of England*, London, n.d., pp. 154–5.
8 Jacobs, J., *English Fairy Tales*, London, 1890, pp. 48–50.
9 Chambers, R., *Popular Rhymes of Scotland*, London and Edinburgh, 1870, pp. 53–5. For full text see Chapter Eleven.

Chapter 4 Cats and Other Creatures as Friends or Foes

1 *Grimm's Fairy Tales*, edited by James Stern, London, 1948, pp. 144–8.
2 Campbell, J. F., *Popular Tales of the West Highlands*, London, 1890, vol. I, pp. 199–202.
3 Kennedy, Patrick, *Legendary Fictions of the Irish Celts*, London, 1891, pp. 4–11.
4 Massignon, Genevieve, *The Folktales of France*, Folktales of the World, Chicago, 1968, pp. 179–81.
5 Owen, Elias, *Welsh Folk-Lore*, Oswestry, 1896, Norwood Editions, 1973, pp. 323–4, 'The Heron, the Cat and the Bramble'.
6 Dawkins, R. M., *Modern Greek Folktales*, Oxford, 1953, p. 40, 'The Grateful Animals and the Talisman'.

7 There are Russian, Lithuanian and Lappish versions of this tale, to which no Type has been assigned, and only one motif, K.815.15 'Cat lures young foxes with music. Kills them'.

8 Murphy, M. J., *Now You're Talking*, Belfast, 1975, p. 140.

9 Seki, Keigo, *Folktales of Japan*, Folktales of the World, Chicago, 1963, p. 25.

10 Iremonger, L., *West Indian Folk-tales*, London, 1956, pp. 59–64.

Chapter 5 Good Luck and Bad Luck

1 Henderson, William, *Folk-Lore from the Northern Counties of England and the Borders*, F.L.S., London, 1879, pp. 207.

2 Radford, E. and M. A., *Encyclopedia of Superstitions*, edited and revised by Christina Hole, London, 1961, p. 87.

3 Briggs, K. M. and Tongue, R. L., *Folktales of England*, Folktales of the World, London, 1965, p. 65.

4 Radford and Hole, *Encyclopedia of Superstitions*, p. 87.

5 Ibid.

6 Trevelyan, Mary, *Folk-Lore and Folk Stories of Wales*, London, 1909, p. 80.

7 Henderson, W., *Folk-Lore from the Northern Counties*, p. 207.

8 Ibid.

9 Addy, S. O., *Household Tales, with Other Traditional Remains*, London, 1895, p. 68.

10 Henderson, W., *Folk-Lore from the Northern Counties*, p. 206.

11 Spence, John, *Shetland Folk-Lore*, Lerwick, 1899, p. 113.

12 Hulme, F. E., *Natural History Lore and Legend*, London, 1895, p. 191.

13 Trevelyan, Mary, *Folk-Lore and Folk Stories of Wales*, p. 80.

14 Radford and Hole, *Encyclopedia of Superstitions*, p. 87.

15 Ibid.

16 Trevelyan, Mary, *Folk-Lore and Folk Stories of Wales*, p. 80. 'If cats suck the breath of babes the latter will die.'

17 Owen, Elias, *Welsh Folk-Lore*, Oswestry, 1876. Reprinted by Norwood Editions, Norwood, Pa, 1973, pp. 341–2.

18 Radford and Hole, *Encyclopedia of Superstitions*, pp. 87–8.

19 Ibid., p. 88.

20 Henderson, W., *Folk-Lore from the Northern Counties*, p. 149.

21 Ibid., p. 207.

22 Radford and Hole, *Encyclopedia of Superstitions*, p. 88.

23 Ibid.

24 Spence, John, *Shetland Folk-Lore*, pp. 144–6.
25 Hulme, F. E., *Natural History Lore and Legend*, pp. 190–1.
26 Owen, E., *Welsh Folk-Lore*, p. 341.
27 Tongue, Ruth, *Somerset Folklore*, F.L.S., County Folklore VIII, London, 1965, p. 51.
28 Radford and Hole, *Encyclopedia of Superstitions*, pp. 86 and 55–6.

Chapter 6 Witches and their Familiars

1 Pitcairn, Robert, *Criminal Trials in Scotland from A.D. 1488–1634*, Edinburgh, 1833, vol. I, pt II, pp. 51–8. Betty Dunlop of Lyne in Ayrshire was tried and condemned to be burned in 1567.
2 Harsnet, S., *Declaration of Egregious Popish Impostures*, London, 1603, p. 136.
3 Porter, Enid, *The Folklore of East Anglia*, London, 1944, p. 145.
4 Gifford, George, *A Dialogue Concerning Witches and Witchcraftes*, Shakespeare Association Facsimile No. 1, Oxford University Press, 1931, p.B.5.
5 Fairfax, Edward, 'A Discourse of Witchcraft as it was acted in the Family of Mr. Edward Fairfax of Fuystone in the County of York in the Year 1621.' The manuscript printed in the *Miscellanies* of the Philobiblon Society, No. 5, 1858–9.
6 Hopkins, Matthew, *The Discovery of Witches*, London, 1647. This trial was held at Chelmsford, and the date of Hopkins's evidence was 25 March 1645. Altogether thirty-two women were indicted, of whom nineteen were hanged and three died in prison before the trial.
7 These devils were first described by her little stepson, Thomas Rabbet. This is an early example of evidence brought by children against their parents. It was this trial which inspired Reginald Scot to write his *Discoverie of Witchcraft*.
8 Goodcole, H., *The Wonderful Discoverie of Elizabeth Sawyer, a Witch, late of Edmonton*, London, 1621. This pamphlet, written by the Chaplain of Newgate is the source of the play by Dekker, Rowley & Ford, 1658.
9 This was in 1612 during the First Lancashire Witch Trials. The pamphlet describing it is a sober one, by the clerk of the court, Thomas Potts, *The Wonderful Discoverie of Witches in the Countie of Lancaster*, 1613.
10 Fairfax, E., 'A Discourse of Witchcraft'. A good article on Edward Fairfax, with the drawings of the familiars, is to be found in *The*

Encyclopedia of Witchcraft and Demonology, Robins, R. H., London, 1959, pp. 189–90.

11 *The Encyclopedia of Witchcraft and Demonology*, pp. 88–92 gives a full account of the First Chelmsford Witch Trial 1566 with extracts from the pamphlet describing it.

12 Hole, Christina, *A Mirror of Witchcraft*, London, 1957, p. 69. Other extracts from the accounts of Jane Wenham's trial are to be found on pp. 100–2, and pp. 22 and 89.

13 Hutchinson, Francis, *An Historical Essay Concerning Witchcraft*, London, 1718.

14 Notestein, Wallace, *A History of Witchcraft in England from 1558–1718*. For the end of the witch trials see Chapters XIII and XIV.

15 Rawling, M., *The Folklore of the Lake District*, London, 1976, pp. 26–7.

16 Barrett, W. H., *More Tales of the Fens*, edited by Enid Porter, London, 1964, pp. 111–18.

17 Ibid., pp. 129–32.

18 Hunt, Robert, *Popular Tales of the West of England*, London, 1830, pp. 326–7.

Chapter 7   Shape-Shifters

1 Henderson, *Notes on the Folk-lore of the Northern Counties of England and the Borders*, London, 1879, p. 208. The story is quoted from *Popular Tales and Traditions from Swedish, Danish and German*, vol. III, p. 26 and is from Eiderstadt in North Germany.

2 Heywood, Thomas, *Dramatic Works*, London, 1874. For comment see Briggs, K. M., *Pale Hecate's Team*, London, 1962, pp. 101–5.

3 Henderson, W., *Notes on the Folk-Lore*, p. 209.

4 Ibid., p. 206.

5 Owen, E., *Welsh Folk-Lore*, Norwood Editions, 1973, Oswestry, 1896, p. 224.

6 Arthur, H., *A Forgotten Heritage*, Edinburgh, 1973, p. 51.

7 Pitcairn, Robert, *Ancient Criminal Trials in Scotland*, Edinburgh, 1833, vol. III, pt II, pp. 602–16.

8 Simpson, Jacqueline, *Folklore of Sussex*, London, 1975, p. 70.

9 *Doctor Lamb's Darling*, London, 1653, pp. 4–5.

10 Knopf, Lewis, trans. by Henry Jones, F.L.S., London, 1889.

11 Harris, *Uncle Remus*, London, 1901, pp. 254–64.

12 Stewart, Grant, *Popular Superstitions of the Highlands of Scotland*, London, 1823, Ward Lock reprint, 1970, p. 205.

13 Ibid, pp. 184–9.
14 Ibid., pp. 189–98.
15 Craigie, W. A., *Scandinavian Folk-Lore*, Paisley and London, 1896. 'Odin pursues the Elf Women', pp. 24–5.
16 Chase, R., *Grandfather Tales*, USA, 1948, pp. 162–9.

Chapter 8   Fairytales: People under Spells

1 *The Types of the Folktale*, Antti Aarne (F.F. Communications no. 3), translated and enlarged by Stith Thompson, 2nd Revision Helsinki, 1961. Type 545 B 'Puss in Boots' p. 194.
2 Dasent, G. W., *Popular Tales from the Norse*, Edinburgh, 1903, pp. 295–302.
3 Craigie, W. A., *Scandinavian Folk-Lore*, Paisley and London, 1896, pp. 58–9, 61–2.
4 D'Aulnoy, *Fairy Tales by the Countess D'Aulnoy*, translated by J. R. Planché, London, n.d. (circa 1910), pp. 337–66.
5 Lang, A., *The Brown Fairy Book*, London, 1904, pp. 256–62. The adaptation is a little careless, for in one place the teller says that Ingibjörg fell asleep at once, and later on that she had been too frightened to sleep. This last embroidery could be left out in re-telling the story.

Chapter 9   Benevolent Cats in Fairytales

1 Buchan, Peter, *Ancient Scottish Tales*, an unpublished collection made by Peter Buchan, Norwood Editions, Darby, Pa., 1973, pp. 51–2.
2 Thorpe, B., *Yule-Tide Stories*, Bohn Library, London, 1884, pp. 97–112.
3 Lang, Andrew, *The Crimson Fairy Book*, London, 1935, pp. 340–9.
4 Ibid., 'The Cottager and his Cat' (*Islandische Märchen*) pp. 174–7.

Chapter 10   Monstrous Cats

1 'The Vulgate Merlin' is one part of a large collection of Arthurian matter compiled from the earlier writings. It is generally thought

to have been put together in the third decade of the thirteenth century and is composed of five branches: An early *History of the Grail*, *Merlin*, a *Lancelot*, a *Quest of the Grail* and *Mort Artur*. The three last are said to have been written by Walter Map. Chambers, E. K., *Arthur of Britain*, London, 1927, pp. 158–63.

2 Wilde, Lady (Speranza), *Ancient Legends, Mystic Charms and Super-stitions of Ireland*, vol. II, London, 1887, pp. 37–40.
For further details about the *Cuchulling Saga* see Hull, Eleanor, *The Cuchulling Saga*, London, 1898.

3 Tongue, Ruth, 'The Four-Eyed Cat' is to be found reproduced in Chapter Five.

4 Henderson, George, *Survivals in Beliefs Among the Celts*, Glasgow, 1911, pp. 108–9.

5 Griffith, E. M., 'The Heart of Down', *The Ulster Tatler*.

Chapter 11   Nursery Tales and Amusements

1 Chambers, Robert, *Popular Rhymes of Scotland*, London and Edinburgh, 1870, pp. 26–7.

2 Jacobs, Joseph, *English Fairy Tales*, London, 1890, pp. 48–50.

3 Chambers, Robert, *Popular Rhymes of Scotland*, pp. 53–4.

4 Ibid., pp. 54–5.

5 Halliwell, J. O., *Nursery Rhymes and Nursery Tales of England*, London and New York, n.d., pp. 114–5. A Hebrew version from Sepher Haggadah is given by Halliwell as a preface to this, pp. 112–13.

6 Chambers, Robert, *Popular Rhymes of Scotland*, pp. 55–6.

7 Halliwell, J. O., *Nursery Rhymes*, p. 86.

8 Ibid.

9 Crane, Walter, *The Baby's Bouquet*, London and New York, n.d., p. 47.

10 Halliwell, J. O., *Nursery Rhymes*, p. 87.

11 Chambers, Robert, *Popular Rhymes of Scotland*, p. 22.

12 Ibid., pp. 31–2.

13 *More Than Twice 55 Popular Songs* (songbook in the 1930s).

14 Chambers, Robert, *Popular Rhymes of Scotland*, p. 105.

15 Ibid., p. 26.

16 Rackham, Arthur, *Mother Goose*, London, n.d., p. 37.

17 MacTaggart, *Gallovidian Encyclopedia*, F.L.S., 1851. Quoted in Alice Gomme's *Traditional Games of England, Scotland and Ireland*, 2 vols, London, 1894, vol II, pp. 256–9.

18 Gomme, Alice, *Traditional Games*, vol. I.
19 Ibid., vol. II, pp. 294–5.
20 Ibid., vol. I, pp. 61–3, an account of the playing of 'Cat's Cradle', with diagrams of the seven forms into which it can be manipulated.

Chapter 12   Cats in Modern Literary Folklore

1 Yonge, C. M., *The Lances of Lynwood*, London, 1891, Chapter VII.
2 Scott, Walter, *Ivanhoe*, Edinburgh, 1820. The trial of Rebecca, the daughter of Isaac the Jew, as a witch, after which Brian de Bois Guilbert was forced to take the lists as her accuser, occurs in Chapter XXXVII. The witchcraft trial is an anachronism. It is almost a century too early.
3 Ewing, J. H., 'The Brownies' (1870) and 'Lob-Lie-by-the-Fire' (1874) follow essentially the same plot, of an old house, traditionally haunted by a lobbish spirit, and has its place supplied by a helpful pair of children or an adopted boy. 'Amelia and the Dwarfs', which is in the same volume as 'The Brownies', is founded on the changeling legend. In this tale it is a spoilt child who is stolen to be reformed, but the reform proves so successful that the fairies are anxious to keep her. The tale is so arranged that it is possible to interpret Amelia's experiences as a delirious dream.
4 Masefield, John, *Midnight Folk*, London, 1927, 5th reprint 1963.
5 Ibid., pp. 12–15.
6 Ibid., pp. 20–2.
7 White, T. H., *The Sword in the Stone*, Glasgow, 1938; paperback edition, Fontana 1978.
8 Gray, Nicholas Stuart, *The Stone Cage*, London, 1963, 2nd Edition 1972.
9 Ibid., pp. 11–12.
10 Ibid., pp. 89–90.
11 Ibid., pp. 90–1.
12 Ibid., p. 246.
13 Gray, Nicholas Stuart, *Over the Hills to Fabylon*, Oxford, 1968, Chapter II.
14 Lewis, C. S., *The Magician's Nephew*, London, 1955; 3rd edition, 1960, pp. 112–16.
15 Lewis, C. S., *The Last Battle*, London, 1956.
16 Ibid., pp. 110–12.
17 Lang, A., *My Own Fairy Book*, London, n.d.

18 Ibid., pp. 91–4.
19 De la Mare, Walter, *Broomsticks and Other Tales*, London, 1925.
20 Ibid., p. 134.
21 Holding, E. S., *Miss Kelly*, London, 1948.
22 Ibid., pp. 6–7.
23 Ibid., p. 60.
24 Potter, Beatrix, *The Tailor of Gloucester*, London, 1903 (1st edition), pp. 38–42.
25 Ibid., pp. 42–6.
26 Warner, Sylvia Townsend, *Lolly Willowes*, 1st edition London, 1926; paperback, Women's Press, London, 1978.
27 Ibid., 1978, pp. 168–9.

List of Books Quoted and Cited

Addy, S. O., *Household Tales: Traditional Remains of York, Lincoln, Derby and Nottingham*, Nutt, London, 1895.

Aitken, Hannah, *A Forgotten Heritage*, Scottish Academic Press, Edinburgh, 1973.

Anglicus, Bartholomew, *De Proprietate Rerum* (thirteenth century), translated by John Trevisa for Sir Thomas, Lord of Berkeley in 1397. *Philologus* the main source. See *Medieval Lore* by Robert Steele, King's Classics, London, 1905, for bibliographical detail.

Aubrey, John, *Remaines of Gentilisme and Judaisme*, London, 1686–7.

Aubrey, John, *Miscellanies*, London, 1696 (first edition).

Barrett, W. H., *More Tales from the Fens*, Routledge & Kegan Paul, London, 1964.

Billson, Charles James, *The County Folk-Lore of Leicestershire and Rutland*, Folklore Society, No. 3, 1895.

Braune, David, *Japanische Märchen und Sagen*, translated in Lang's *Pink Fairy Book*.

Briggs, K. M., *A Dictionary of British Folk-Tales in the English Language*, 4 vols, Routledge & Kegan Paul, London, 1970–1.

Briggs, K. M. and Tongue, R. L., *Folktales of England* (Folktales of the World), Routledge & Kegan Paul, London, 1965.

Buchan, Peter, *Ancient Scottish Tales. An Unpublished Collection Made by Peter Buchan*, Facsimile by Norwood Editions, Darby, Pa, 1973.

Campbell, J. F., *Popular Tales of the West Highlands*, 4 vols, Gardner, London, 1890.

Chambers, Robert, *Popular Rhymes of Scotland*, Chambers, London and Edinburgh, 1870 (first edition 1841).

Chase, Richard, *Grandfather Tales*, Houghton Mifflin Co., Boston, USA, 1948.

Crane, Walter, *Baby's Bouquet*, Routledge, London, 1879.

Dasent, G. W., *Tales from the Norse*, Douglas, Edinburgh, 1903 (first edition 1868).

D'Aulnoy, *Fairy Tales by the Countess d'Aulnoy*, translated by J. R. Planché, London and New York, n.d. (*circa* 1911).

Dawkins, R. M., *Modern Greek Folktales*, Clarendon, Oxford, 1953.

De la Mare, Walter, *Broomsticks*, Constable, London, 1925.

Degh, Linda, *Folktales of Hungary* (Folktales of the World), University of Chicago Press, 1965.

The Denham Tracts, Folk-Lore Society, London, 1895, vol. II.

Diodorus Siculus (First century BC), Sicilian historian, English translation The Historical Library London 1700. Animal worship in Egypt I, pp. 43–7. A World History. *The Historical Library of Diodorus Siculus* (Thirty years to write 40 volumes), Historian's History of the World, Vol. I.

Eberard, W., *Folktales of China* (Folktales of the World), University of Chicago Press, 1965.

Ewing, J. H., *The Brownies and Other Tales*, SPCK, London, 1920.

Ewing, J. H., *Lob-Lie-by-the-Fire and other Stories*, SPCK, London, 1923.

Fairfax, Edward, 'A Discourse of Witchcraft as it was acted in the family of Mr. Edward Fairfax of Fuystone in the County of York in the Year 1621'. Manuscript in the British Museum, illustrated by Miles Gale, Rector of Keighley, with drawings of the witches' familiars. Printed by Philobiblon Society, *Miscellanies*, No. 5, 1858–9.

Gifford, George, *A Dialogue Concerning Witches and Witchcraftes*, 1593, Shakespeare Facsimiles No. 1. Sheet B.5.

Gomme, Alice, *A Dictionary of British Folk-Lore*, Part I: Traditional Games, 2 vols, Nutt, London, 1898.

Gray, Nicholas Stuart, *The Stone Cage*, Dobson, London, 1963 (2nd edition 1972).

Gray, Nicholas Stuart, *Over the Hills to Fabylon*, Dobson, London, 1968.

Griffith, E. H., 'The Heart of Down', *The Ulster Tatler*, n.d.

Grimm, *Grimm's Fairy Tales*, translated and edited by Margaret Hunt and James Stern, Routledge & Kegan Paul, London, 1948.

Grimm, Jacob, *Teutonic Mythology*, translated by J. S. Stallybrass, 4 vols, Bell, London, 1882–8, vol. I.

Halliwell, J. O., *Nursery Rhymes and Nursery Tales of England*, Smith, London, n.d. (*c.* 1858) (first edition 1849).

Harris, Joel Chandler, *Uncle Remus*, Grant Richards, London, 1901.

Harsnet, S., *A Declaration of Egregious Popish Impostures*, London, 1603.

Hartland, E. S., *English Fairy and Folk Tales*, Walter Scott Press, London, 1893.

Henderson, George, *Survivals in Belief among the Celts*, James Maclehose & Sons, Glasgow, 1911.

Henderson, William, *Folklore from the Northern Counties of England and the Borders*, Folk-Lore Society, London, 1879.

Herodotus (quoted in Larousse. Account of the festive pilgrimage to Bubastis in April), Historians History of the World I.

Heywood, Thomas, *The Late Lancashire Witches*, London, 1634.

Holding, Elizabeth S., *Miss Kelly*, Michael Joseph, London, 1948.

Hole, Christina, *A Mirror of Witchcraft*, Chatto & Windus, London, 1957.

Hopkins, Matthew, *The Discovery of Witches*, London, 1647, pamphlet written by Hopkins, 'Witch-finder General', when his methods began to be suspected; he died in 1646.

Hulme, F. E., *Natural History: Lore and Legend*, Quaritch, London, 1895.

Hunt, Robert, *Popular Romances of the West of England*, London, 1930 (reprint of 3rd edition, Chatto, London, 1881).

Hutchinson, Francis, *An Historical Essay concerning Witchcraft*, London, 1718.

Iremonger, Lucille, *West Indian Folk-Tales*, Harrap, London, 1956.

Jacobs, J., *English Fairy Tales*, Nutt, London, 1890.

Jones, Henry and Knopf, Lewes, *The Folk-Tales of the Magyars*, Folklore Society, London, 1889.

Kennedy, Patrick, *Legendary Fictions of the Irish Celts*, Macmillan, London, 1866.

Lang, Andrew, *The Brown Fairy Book*, Longmans, London, 1904.

Lang, Andrew, *The Crimson Fairy Book*, Longmans, London, 1935.

Lang, Andrew, *The Pink Fairy Book*, Longmans, London, 1936, translated from David Braune, *Japanische Märchen und Sagen*, Leipzig, Wilhelm Friedrich.

Lang, Andrew, *My Own Fairy Book*, Arrowsmith, Bristol, n.d.

Larousse, *Encyclopedia of Mythology*, London, 1959.

Lewis, C. S., *The Last Battle*, Bodley Head, London, 1956.

Mackenzie, Donald A., *Scottish Folk Lore and Folk Life*, Blackie, London and Glasgow, 1935.

MacTaggart, *Gallovidian Encyclopedia* (cited in Lady Gomme's *Dictionary of Traditional Games*).

Malleus Malificarem, Leyden, 1486. The most sinister and influential book about witchcraft, widely translated (first English translation 1584).

Masefield, John, *The Midnight Folk*, Heinemann, London, 1927 (5th reprint 1963).

Massignon, Genevieve, *Folktales of France* (Folktales of the World), University of Chicago Press, 1968.

Michaelis-Jena, Ruth and Ratcliff, Arthur, *New Tales from Grimm*, Edinburgh, 1960.

Murphy, Michael J., *Now You're Talking*, Belfast, 1975.

Murray, Margaret, *The God of the Witches*, Low, London, 1933.

Opie, Iona and Peter, *The Oxford Dictionary of Nursery Rhymes*, OUP, London, 1951.

O'Sullivan, Sean, *Folktales of Ireland* (Folktales of the World), University of Chicago Press, 1966.

Owen, Elias, *Welsh Folk-Lore*, Norwood Editions, Norwood Pa, 1973 (facsimile of 1896 edition, Woodall, Hinshall, Oswestry).

Pitcairn, R., *Ancient Criminal Trials in Scotland*, Edinburgh, 1833, vol. I, part II, pp. 51–8, The Trial of Bessie Dunlop (1576).

Porter, Enid, *The Folklore of East Anglia*, Batsford, London, 1974.

Potter, Beatrix, *The Tailor of Gloucester*, Warne, London, 1903.

Rackham, Arthur, *Mother Goose. The Old Nursery Rhymes*.

Radford, E. and M., *Encyclopedia of Superstitions*, edited and revised by Christina Hole, Hutchinson, London, 1961.

Ransome, Arthur, *Old Peter's Russian Tales*, Nelson, London, 1935.

Rawling, Marjorie, *Folklore of the Lake District*, London, 1976.

Scott, Walter, *Ivanhoe*, Edinburgh, 1819.

Scott, Walter, *Minstrelsy of the Scottish Border*, 4 vols, Edinburgh, 1801 and 1830, edited by T. F. Henderson.

Seki, Keigo, *Folktales of Japan* (Folktales of the World), University of Chicago Press, 1963.

Simpson, Jacqueline, *Folklore of Sussex*, London, 1973 (*The Sussex County Magazine* 1935).

Spence, John, *Shetland Folk-Lore*, Johnson, Lerwick, 1899.

Spence, Lewis, *Myths and Legends of Ancient Egypt*, London, 1917.

Stewart, W. Grant, *Popular Superstitions of the Highlanders of Scotland*, Constable, London, 1823; Ward Lock reprint, London, 1970.

Tongue, Ruth L., *Forgotten Folk-Tales of the English Counties*, Routledge & Kegan Paul, London, 1970.

Topsell, Edward, *Historie of Four-Footed Beastes*, London, 1607.

Trevelyan, Mary, *Folk-Lore and Folk-Stories of Wales*, London, 1909.

Vulgate Merlin, thirteenth-century prose romance. 'King Arthur and the Cat' quoted by Lady Wilde in *Ancient Legends of Ireland*, vol. II, pp. 37–40.

Warner, Sylvia Townsend, *Lolly Willowes*, Chatto & Windus, London, 1926; The Women's Press, London, 1978.

White, T. H., *The Sword in the Stone*, Collins, London, 1938.

Wilde, Lady, *Ancient Legends, Mystic Charms, of Ireland*, Ward, London, 1887, 2 vols.

Wolkstein, Diane, *The Magic Orange Tree and other Haitian Folktales*, New York, 1978.

Yonge, Charlotte H., *The Lances of Lynwood*, Macmillan, London, 1891.

Zong-in-Sob, *Folk-Tales from Korea* (Folktales of the World), London, 1952.

Index

217